International Green Politics

edited by Sabine von Mering
and Sarah Halpern-Meekin

The Center for German and European Studies
in cooperation with the
Heinrich Böll Foundation, Washington, D.C.

Brandeis University
Waltham, Massachusetts

ISBN 0-9620545-4-2

Office of Publications
©2002 Brandeis University
S140

Table of Contents

Preface

In March 2001, President Bush declared that his government would not support the regulation of carbon dioxide emissions from U.S. power plants despite his campaign promise to do so and that he would not ratify the Kyoto Protocol on Global Warming. The Protocol, which had been signed by 80 countries including the United States, calls for drastic reduction of CO2 emissions worldwide.

The political implications of Bush's withdrawal as he faces a European Union with strong Green party representation spurred us to organize a conference on politics and the environment. On November 11, 2001, the Center for German and European Studies at Brandeis University in collaboration with the Heinrich Böll Foundation, Washington, D.C., hosted the International Conference on Green Politics. The conference was co-sponsored by the Environmental Studies Program, and the Sustainable International Development Program at Brandeis University. Participants included Green politicians, activists, and scholars from around the world.

The goal of the conference was to examine Green politics on the national, international, and global level. The conference was divided into three parts, European Greens in Government: Challenges to Green Politics; Green Politics in the United States; and Greens and Global Environmental Politics. This volume offers a selection of the articles presented at the conference.

The Center for German and European Studies thanks the Heinrich Böll Foundation and its Director, Mr. Sascha Müller-Kraenner, for the generous support that made the conference and this publication possible. We also thank *National Civic Review* for permission to reprint the article written by Theresa Amato and Ralph Nader.

Texas alone, with a population of 30 million, emits more CO_2 than 93 developing countries added together, with a combined population of nearly one billion people.
ECO Publication 1998

Politics can also be the art of the impossible
Vaclav Havel

Introduction
Sabine von Mering

Environmental movements have been around since the late 19th century. They have fought logging in Oregon and deforestation in the Amazon region, nuclear power plants in Germany and Russia, and whaling by Japan and Norway. They have focused the world's attention on the fragility of the ozone layer and biodiversity. They have long warned of the potential dangers of global climate change. In a move from protest to power, environmentalists have made an appearance in politics proper since the late 1970s. Entering parliament with flowers in their hands and sneakers on their feet, the Greens, who were at first smiled upon as "tree-huggers" by political elites, became a self-evident part of the political spectrum in many European countries. Yet until today the Green Parties and their voters continue to debate whether representation in parliament and government participation are indeed the best way to address the vast array of environmental challenges.

Is a Green politician an oxymoron? Greens have traditionally been against those in power, because in their view politicians cling to power at all cost. Some argue that the environment would be better served if Greens directed their energy to their traditional role of

3

non-parliamentary opposition. Then their message would not be watered-down by compromise. That assumes that environmental threats can either be addressed without the help of governmental action, or that pressures from protest movements will force traditional parties to absorb the issues in time.

What are Green politics and how do Green movements become parties? Can the need to protect the environment be addressed by successful party politics? What characterizes Green parties in Europe and how are they different from environmental movements in the US? How do Greens join forces in international networks? While in the multiparty systems of democratic Europe Greens have become small coalition partners, the more recently founded US Green party is struggling against a cemented two-party system. Are existing environmental protection laws and the Environmental Protection Agency successful instruments to counter the effects of pollution in the United States? Polluters can be forced into compliance by legislation and litigation. But stricter laws at home invite corporations to move operations abroad. Consequently, two sides of globalization emerge, as environmentalists begin to collaborate globally against multinational corporate polluters. To examine all these issues within a framework of international comparison was the task of the International Conference on Green Politics, held at Brandeis University on November 11, 2001.

The contributors to this volume, which collects a selection of the papers presented at the conference, bring specific expertise to the questions. They are politicians, scholars, and activists working on four different continents. They critically examine the possibilities for political solutions to today's environmental challenges from a variety of historical, legal, and strategic perspectives. What emerges from the discussions that took place on November 11 is the growing consensus that environmental concerns form an integral part of a range of political issues from agriculture to social policy and transportation. The panelists also pointed out the risks this integration poses for Green politicians. On the one hand, as recent developments in the German Green Party have shown, Green voters have idealistic expectations of their elected officials. Unless these expectations immediately translate into successful political action on behalf of the environment, Green parties in government lose their support. On the other hand, if voting Green remains primarily a protest vote, the political consequences are dubious. Thus many Democratic voters in the United States, who hold Ralph Nader's campaign for president responsible for Al Gore's defeat, are indirectly blaming Green voters for the Bush Administration's anti-environment policies. Could Americans embrace a European-style coalition government? While voters may wonder how best to increase their government's attention to environmental issues, Green politicians here are strengthening their efforts on local and regional levels.

While the need to preserve clean drinking water, wildlife, rainforests, and a healthy climate unites people around the globe, Green politics remains predominantly local, often initiated by protest against a particular environmental threat, such as a toxic waste site or regional over-fishing. At the same time Green politics are naturally transnational, as pollution does not stop at national borders. This has finally been recognized in the context of global warming. In December 2000, members of international delegations meeting to prepare the ratification of the Kyoto Protocol (including the United States) agreed that the global climate is changing as a result of increasing CO2 emissions. They also agreed that the speed of climate change depends on the rate at which we add additional green house gases to the atmosphere. The dramatic breakaway of a massive iceberg in Antarctica observed on March 23, 2002, proved "an ominous reminder that there is no guarantee that changes...caused by global warming will occur at a predictable or uniform rate."(Boston Globe Editorial, March 29, 2002). Some areas will be affected sooner and more heavily than others.

That the threats to the environment are also contributing to silencing those who are least able to defend themselves is incontrovertible according to Grace Akumu's and Ari Hershowitz's assessments. The poorest countries in the world are already facing the highest costs of global warming, just as "environmental racism" affects poor minorities forced to live with hazardous waste facilities in their neighborhoods in industrialized countries. The U.S. economy is the strongest in the world. Yet President Bush claims it cannot afford the reduction of greenhouse gases at the levels required by the Kyoto Protocol. Others claim that the country is perfectly able to meet these expectations. As the Natural Resources Defense Council observes: "two comprehensive government studies have shown that it is possible to reduce greenhouse pollution to levels called for in the Kyoto agreement without harming the economy."(NRDC website) Indeed, the United States resistance to Kyoto is actually based on quite a different threat: The fear of the potential competition of the growing economies of developing nations that would not have to commit to the same levels of restraint at this point.

As long as environmental protection is only viewed as a nuisance by the most influential corporate leaders and the general public alike, politicians will lack the power to make necessary changes happen. Yet despite the fact that most electricity in the United States is still generated by burning fossil fuels such as coal, natural gas, and oil, even large oil companies have actually begun to invest in "Renewables." While the oil industry may just be paying lip service, sectors of the international economy which are directly affected by environmental threats have become forerunners in sustainable development, as the example of the re-insurance sector demonstrates, "dangers to healthy economies can arise from many quarters, including threats to food security, water security, and health" writes Rolf Gerling, of Gerling Group of Insurance Companies in his introduction to *Climate Change and the Financial Sector*, edited by the renowned scholar of global warming Jeremy Leggett (1996). Above all, the United States needs the political creativity and determination to implement incentives for saving energy. As the U.S. Senate is debating the Bush administration's energy bill we witness the need for informed advocacy on behalf of the environment at the highest levels of government. The Globe Editorial concludes aptly: "The country would be better off with no new energy bill at all than with one that backs more use of fossil fuels and gives Americans a false sense that their government is addressing global warming. It isn't."

Brandeis University seeks to promote the search for truth in the name of social justice. The complex challenges to international Green politics frequently highlight the competition between social justice and sustainable development; seeking to improve people's conditions of life through economic growth, while limiting the damage from economic development. As the articles in this volume confirm, Green politicians were the first to introduce radical new initiatives not just in the area of the environment. They also advocate other causes, from gender equality to peace activism, from the fight against poverty to the ethical treatment of animals. In all these areas they challenge traditional political parties. This volume hopes to stimulate debate about how Greens successfully mobilize their voters and advocate the right direction for change, locally and globally, or, as they say, *glocally*.

I. European Greens in Government: Challenges to Green Politics

A Post-Westphalian Party: The German Greens
Carl Lankowski[*]

In March 1998 I happened to be in the German federal
state of North Rhine Westphalia and noticed a very short
newspaper report about a convocation in the Münster
Rathaus to commemorate the 350th anniversary of the
signing of the Treaty of Westphalia. Though attended
by an impressive delegation of notables it did not attract
participation by the most senior officials of government
and passed with little fanfare. That treaty is generally
taken as a major turning point in European and world
history, the birth of the modern state system based on
territorially defined, sovereign entities. Endemic to the
further development of the Westphalian system is the
concept of national interest. In the era of mass politics
inaugurated in the latter part of the 19th century states
could become altogether too self-referential, deforming
national interest into a pathology that twice led to world
war. After the second global conflagration and loss of
life of more than 50 million human beings, Westphalian
principles were balanced by massive innovation of global
international organizations under the UN umbrella.
Meanwhile, Europe's political collapse paved the way for
de-colonization and the worldwide spread of collective
self-determination based on the Westphalian territorial
principle. At the same time, Western Europe launched
the experiment of regional integration. All this unfolded
under the cold war bi-hegemony of the continental
superpowers. By the time the USSR collapsed, the
European Union was already on course to becoming

9

the economic superpower it is today. Revolutions in transportation and especially communications supported economic globalization. North/South stratification became a major issue in this context. Other transnational processes and a battery of new, post-cold war global issues emerged: migration, the environment, disease, organized crime, and transnational terrorism. In short, by the time Westphalia was being commemorated, the world had passed into a post-Westphalian condition.

Post-Westphalian refers to a transitional condition in which the template of nation-states continues to define the basic structure of world politics, even as the social, economic, political and cultural infrastructures have metamorphosized so as to attenuate national control. In particular, policing this "new world order" still requires national military action on occasion, albeit in coalitions of the willing, as is dramatically on display in Afghanistan, Bosnia and Kosovo at the time of this writing.

Enter the German "68 generation." As progeny of those directly experiencing the Third Reich, West German 68ers were bound to be a unique political breed. Already in the 1960s the intensely felt sentiments *nie wieder Krieg* ("never again war") and *nie wieder Ausschwitz* ("never again Auschwitz") produced an extra-parliamentary opposition in the Federal Republic's fledgling democracy. These circumstances gave a special twist to the broad program of societal reform for which the 68ers put their collective shoulder to the wheel of history. Though they ultimately plumped for a long march through the institutions, embracing electoral and parliamentary arenas, they started not with a desire to occupy the state, but to transform (German) society.

Rejection of their elders encouraged them to adumbrate an alternative vision that by-passed the state, focusing on local action in a global framework. This process was undertaken during the 1970s, culminating in a decisive break with left-wing sectarians after the Red Army Fraction (RAF) Mogadishu/Stammheim debacle of October 1977. The first local and regional Green Parties in Germany were founded at that time.

Having chosen the path of electoral politics, their efforts have been crowned with electoral success wherever electoral laws provided them with an initial toehold in office. And at least some have navigated the tricky transition from protest movements to fountains of ideas, and from that stage to participation in governments at the local, federal-state, and since September 1998, the national level. A major question hovers over their efforts now. Has the generation expended its political capital in irrelevancies, or has it managed to transform the conditions of its existence and is it bequeathing a fertile legacy to the successor generations?

I want to suggest that one very important, though little appreciated vantage point on this problem consists in the European dimension.

The 1970s was the decade of the so-called "new" social movements, which—we must remind ourselves— deliberately broke free from the confining yoke of sectarian formations on the traditional left, for the "new politics" they projected into the political arena. Rallying points were the women's movement, the environmental movement, and the peace movement. Both the form and the substance of conventional political action were broken by these novel collective identities. There was the rejection of mass parties belonging to the left wing of the political spectrum, notables parties traditionally associated with the Liberals, and the structurally populist, "people's parties," of post-war origin that belonged to the right and center-right. Movement politics were in this sense an "anti-politics," an assault on the post-war party system as such. Each of the core movements just mentioned challenged entrenched positions of the existing mainstream parties, which not only accommodated themselves to, but actually defined themselves by what Charles Maier called the "politics of productivity" in the cold war setting. In retrospect, anti-politics were not only possible but also progressive because they attached themselves to the evolving conditioning forces of the party landscape.

The decade marked the transition to the 68ers' distinctive party-political contribution, what Herbert Kitschelt labeled the "post-industrial framework party." Very much a creature of the New Left in inspiration, the Greens represented issues that challenged the parameters of the post-war settlement. While a major function of the parties was to sustain cold war divisions, anti-politics challenged the idiom based on economic growth as a solvent to class antagonisms. In some ways, the German Greens proved to be the best exemplars of these developments. The reasons are to be found in the particulars of postwar German development. The main factors include:

• The intensity of the "NIE WIEDER" element among the baby boomers. The intensity of protest in Germany gathered extra force due to the irrepressible recent national past.

- Unavailability of an alternative, such as existed in most of Germany's small country neighbors, of a suitable pre-existing political vehicle on the left. The SPD launched Germany's initially ambitious nuclear power program and continued Germany's role as the lynchpin of NATO, to the point where, too late, SPD activists withdrew support of "their" government, leaving the field free for a shift of governing coalitions between national elections. By then, the SPD was *Staatstragend und Jugendfrei* ("state-supporting and youth-free"). It must be added that one reason for the Greens' success consisted in the serious gap between SPD appeals ("mehr Demokratie wagen" "dare more democracy") and what it actually delivered (nuclear energy, *Radikalenerlass*, NATO allegiance, a gendered understanding of the welfare state that deprived women of the benefits of both political and social citizenship).

The European dimension served as the defining moment of the emergence of the German Greens as a national political party in the 1979 direct elections to the European Parliament. Led by, among others, Petra Kelly, SPD-Die Grünen had the look of a fronde aimed at the European status quo. The anti-nuclear and peace movements had already brought activists from several European countries into contact with each other. They took advantage of this first supranational electoral exercise in Europe by sharply attacking the entire set-up. Twenty years on, it is hard to understand the intensity of the clash. From the point of view of the New Left and its allies, underlying the rosy rhetoric of European integration was the reality of "original sins" of the post-war European settlement: fixation on the ethos of economic growth to the detriment of the environment, technocratic remoteness from the citizens, insensitivity

13

to concerns of women, blind faith in dangerous technologies such as nuclear power, and at the very least a powerful but indirect support for the Atlantic Alliance. In the view of most activists, the cold war was dangerously dependent on the risky policy of deterrence, a policy that in light of technological developments embodied in new, more accurate, shorter-range nuclear missiles, amounted to, as Edward Thompson put it, "exterminism." Theirs was a critique of war as an extension of politics by other means. For it was not only Europe, on whose soil a war using weapons of mass destruction might be fought, that was at risk, but the human species itself. In short, "Brussels" was not only an expression of, but actually a prop supporting the political cartels dominating national politics. The "Rome Treaty" was construed as the symbol of everything the new secular Protestants stood against.

The new politics dimension worked as a catalytic agent to recompose West Germany's political landscape. "Greening" at the national level reverberated powerfully at the supra-national level, facilitating Europeanization of policy in the nascent multi-level, Brussels-oriented system. In Germany's high turnout, proportional representation electoral system, a new dynamic was introduced that compelled the dominant centrist "people's parties" (*Volksparteien*) to take on board themes introduced by the Greens. The lack of a communist party provided an advantage, insofar as German Social Democrats were free to appeal to elements of the new service economy and contribute to the global and post-industrial ethos of the Greens. Initially, this led to disorganization on the left, helping the CDU and FDP to power for 16 years. At the same time, the Maastricht and

Amsterdam Treaty debates have manifested the exposure of the center-right to a nationalist, anti-immigrant, Euro-skeptical agenda.

It was at this point that the policy debate in the upper echelons of the Green Party began to converge with the internationalist vision of much of the Green electorate. German unification, the disintegration of the Soviet Union and the Balkans crisis coursed together to move the party elite away from its anti-Establishment, moralizing pose. It dawned on them that the choice lay not in a hypothetical third way between capitalism and state socialism, nor in designing a European order from scratch, but rather between variants of incremental reforms in actually existing structures.

At the European level, the Greens gradually lent critical support to the EU. The milestones along the way were:

• The direct election and subsequent consolidation of the European Parliament in the Brussels institutional matrix—the Greens joined forces with assorted regionalists to form the GRAEL fraction in the EP from 1984-1989.

• Promulgation of the Single European Market ("Europe-92"), ratified in 1987, which charted the rapidly increasing salience of integration politics. The writing was on the wall: for good or ill, "Europe" would increasingly impact the daily lives of citizens of the member states. "European domestic politics" was hence less a slogan than a fact of life to which one had to adjust.

• Despite the "original sins" of the integration project, new themes corresponding to core programmatic interests of the Greens, were injected into the debate,

15

creating a situation in which it became possible to think of the EC as an arena to use against the national political cartels. Environmental policy is an important instance.

- The end of the cold war and the collapse of the Soviet Union created a situation in which an urgent need arose to define a workable international order in Europe. The density of EC (later EU) institutions provided the most credible framework for advancing the project of taming national rivalries. The unification of Germany posed special problems for the German party and it was not long before, in November 1993, at its Aachen party conference, B-90/Die Grünen shifted their stance fundamentally. Henceforth, the party would stand for radical reform of the EU in the direction of realizing the promise of "European domestic politics" on a platform that insisted on democratization that would bring about an end to the "permissive consensus" underlying the elite-driven Brussels-Member State technocracy, re-routing the EU's economistic course with an intensified environmental and social agenda, and transcending national rivalries in a "working peace system."

None of this would have mattered were it not for the fact that a potential Green electorate existed to support the new realism. The competition for such an electorate focused on a post-68 generation savvy to the limits of state provision in an aging, fiscally challenged, low-employment society. As the tempo of economic globalization picked up, the opening of opportunities became more important than increasingly dubious promises of social insurance. This was a potential electorate that desired to lean forward and outward, engaging in the world, solving its problems, not one that was interested in defending a utopia, however concrete.

Recent public opinion polls bear out this orientation. The Mannheim-based Forschungsgruppe Wahlen's Politbarometer of May 2001 clearly demonstrates the close correlation between rising levels of education and positive perceptions of the EU. The positive correlation is stronger for males than females, for those living in the western as opposed to the eastern Länder. Significantly, of the five parties represented in the Bundestag, those voting for the Greens (with a score of 38%) outranked voters for all other parties. Indicative of the Liberal strain in the Greens' orientation is the fact that the FDP (Liberals) were closest to the Greens in seeing advantages of EU membership (31%). Among socioeconomic groups, "blue collar" respondents were least likely to see advantages to EU membership in the EU in 2001 (12%), in contrast to "white collar" respondents (25%) and the self-employed (35%). Seven months before Euro-currency coins and notes were introduced, an impressive 68% of Green voters thought it was a good thing that the Euro would replace the Deutsche Mark (58% for FDP voters, 47% for SPD voters, 44% for CDU/CSU voters, 33% for PDS voters and 25% for non-voters). All the other correlations discussed for "EU advantages" (sex, region, socioeconomic status, education) also hold for the Euro-currency question. Similarly, the desirability of developing stronger European consciousness in the future varied positively with education level, while education level is inversely correlated with the desirability of greater German consciousness in the future, and German consciousness is correlated positively with age. In short, recent polling data point to an outward-looking, Euro-optimist segment among those most likely to be Green voters.

The political sea change just described is more a promise than a reality, but it has established the Greens as Europe's first "post-Westphalian" party. Not only is the issue-agenda advanced by the Greens tendentially transnational, its EU support strengthens the credibility of the European model of civilizing international relations, an example that has dramatic significance for regions similarly riven by intractable feuds. Not so long ago, during the initial disintegration of Yugoslavia, one Israeli perceptively commented: in the Middle East, if we don't make Brussels, we are likely to make Sarajevo.

In achieving the character of a post-Westphalian party, the Greens have performed an essential historical duty in party-political terms: they provide a standard against which the European policies of the original supporters of European integration can be judged. Of special significance here are the "people's parties" of the center-right. The parties of Adenauer, de Gasperi, Spaak and Schuman must be credited with setting Europe on the path of integration. In particular, the Franco-German rapprochement has been critical to this project through the years, down to and including the European policies of Kohl and Mitterrand, whom we have to thank for the (Maastricht) Treaty on European Union. However, in choosing to respond to the policy imperatives of transnational cooperation with a short-sighted populist, and nationally oriented EU legitimation strategy, these parties have forsaken one of the great challenges of the times: meshing accommodation to globalization with the endangered and hard-won achievements of liberal democracy.

After 9/11, the challenges to the post-Westphalian parties of Europe remain great. In global affairs, clashing sensitivities must be overcome. A mindless anti-Americanism, whether from French nationalists or German pacifists, must give way to a convincing transatlantic strategy for the long transition to the peaceful, tolerant, democratic world order for which so many hope and on which we all depend.

*This commentary expresses the author's analysis and opinions, which are not necessarily shared by the U.S. Department of State.

European Green Party Policy—The Austrian Green Party
Franz Floss

A major difference between American Greens and
European Greens lies in the electoral systems with
which they contend. With the exception of England
and France, the European countries have proportional
electoral systems, and primaries are not known in Europe.
Here the party decides autonomously on the list of
candidates that are placed on the ballot. Consequently,
one finds multi-party systems all over Europe. It is typical
to have three or more parties represented in the national
parliaments. One party with the dominant majority is a
rare situation, and most of the governments are based on
a coalition of several parties. Additionally, because the
state finances the parliamentary parties, they play a much
stronger role in Europe than in the United States.

The development of the Austrian Green Party is similar
to all the other Green Parties in Europe. It was
established in 1986 out of a movement against a nuclear
power plant and it was associated with several peace
movements and some ecological scientists. Initially, we
entered the national parliament with 4.8 percent of the
electoral votes by exceeding an electoral threshold of
4 percent. Since then our typical electoral results were
around 5 percent. In 1999, which was our last national
election, we got 7.4 percent. As for the election to the
European Parliament, our best electoral result is 9.3
percent. In the capital city, Vienna, we got 13 percent
in the election of 2001. After the formation of an
ultra-conservative right wing governmental coalition, the
present opinion polls indicate that our support is 12 to
15 percent.

Austria is a small country with a population of no more than eight million. According to our electoral results, we receive eight million dollars in funds per year from the state. Our party employs more than 120 staff members. There are three press officers in the parliament in Vienna and an additional two in our Vienna city branch. As you will see, timely press releases are very important for us.

Entering the parliament and getting state funding led to a vital change of party policy. The most important impact has been that the parliament has become the main stage for promoting our green policy. Now it is not a question if environmental politics are liked or not, it has become reality that the Members of Parliament (MPs) have major influence on the country's green policy. In other words, the day-to-day policy making has become highly important for the Green Party, not just the general policy statements as in the past. It also implies that we have to broaden and deepen our knowledge to many additional fields, ranging from agriculture to pension rights and from urban planning to food safety. The response to each potential issue, event, and news item must be prompt. In order to have our press release shown on the evening TV news and in the newspapers the next day, we generally have to react to the press releases from other parties before 2 p.m. on the same day. In addition, we have to maintain a good connection to the mass media.

This creates a major problem to our Green Party's guiding principle of grass roots democracy. On the one hand, the MPs have to react quickly, and often on issues which have not been discussed or decided by the rank-and-file-members. On the other hand, a democratic decision made by the members of the whole national party takes a lot of coordination and time. Consequently, the party has to run on two speed levels: the day-to-day political reactions by the MPs and the months or even years long discussion for the party program. The only way to manage this difficult situation is to select our MPs very carefully, to control them with a strong party executive committee (EC) and to trust their political wisdom. With the party executives working all the time, it means that at least some of the EC members have to work fulltime as salaried employees.

The European Green parties are not single-issue parties any more. In their policy, the social and democratic demands are as important as the ecological issues. Sometimes they are even being blamed for neglecting their ecological roots, but in reality it is necessary for them not to limit green policy to pure environmental demands. Environmental successes are inseparably connected with changes in the economy and democracy of the country, therefore sustainable development of the environment, the economy and the democracy are now center issues of our political programs. Fighting unemployment and discrimination against foreigners are equally important to the fight against the Greenhouse Effect.

When Green Parties enter the government, they are—for the time being—minority partners. Staying in the government is full of compromises and it is important to explain this reality to our voters and supporters in advance in the election campaign, otherwise we might create illusions and it will back fire when we are in office. Of equal importance is keeping the rank-and-file members of the party informed and involved in decisions we take as governmental party, otherwise they do not understand why we are being forced to participate in often not so green governmental decisions.

Being in government, we face the problem that normally the larger party and its chancellor gains most of the credit for successes. As the Finnish Green Party has shown in the reelection of their parliament, however, even as a minority partner, it is possible to have good electoral results and gain seats.

We as Green Parties in Europe want to change the society radically, but if only 10-15 percent of the electorate is voting for us, the majority does not want the same radical changes as we do. So, a cautious education process is necessary to align the voters and our interests. The Austrian Green Party is not part of the government now, and we have very little freedom to decide whether we want to participate in a future government. The Social Democratic Party was the ruling party of Austria in the last 25 years and lost the governmental representation only in the last elections. We are fighting against the ultra-conservative right-wing government in Austria, and we would certainly enter serious governmental negotiation talks if we were to win a majority together with the Social Democratic Party in the next election. Any other option would not be understandable for our voters.

Green Politics in France

George Ross

Les Verts, the French Green Party, had an embarrassing moment concerning its candidates for the French Presidential Election of 2002. When Alain Lipietz, the candidate the Greens first nominated, flopped in public and opinion polls, amid intrigue and plots inside the party, his candidacy was revoked and he was replaced by another candidate, Noel Mamère. At first glance this seems to be, as the French would say, *la petite histoire.* The story is well worth recounting, however, because it reveals much about the dilemmas in contemporary Green politics in Europe. Initial successes in the 1980s in making people aware of environmental threats gave Greens serious voice in their national political debates. In time these successes changed the situations in which Greens worked, mixing up environmental issues with the terms upon which Greens might participate in political power.

French Greens produced a political soap opera over summer 2001. In late June a convention of rank-and-file Green Party delegates designated Alain Lipietz, a Green Member of the European Parliament and local Councilor in a Paris suburb, to be the Green candidate in the 2002 Presidential elections. Lipietz's nomination success in narrowly defeating (50.3% of the vote) the pre-convention favorite, Noel Mamère, was a surprise. The new candidate was not an unknown, however, and his credentials were impeccable. Lipietz had graduated second in his class from the prestigious École Polytechnique, one of the rarified schools (along with the École Nationale d'Administration) that have produced French elites for decades. He was also an internationally distinguished economist, one of the leading figures in the French "Regulation School," and the author of several important books. Finally, he had paid his dues many times over as an activist, first, before the Greens coalesced as a political force in the 1980s, in the most creative organizations of the non-Communist Left, and then in the Greens.

On paper Lipietz looked strong.[1] Yet before the press had even written their stories about the Green nomination meeting, political shells began to fall on his head. By early summer, before the French began their massive annual transhumance to holiday destinations, it was clear that Lipietz's every word was being scrutinized and deconstructed for style and content. This was perhaps to be expected in a Presidential campaign in France, where politics becomes sport. What was surprising, however, was how much of this criticism was clearly coming from inside the Green camp itself.

The Green Presidential candidacy was symbolic and important for the party. Lipietz had absolutely no chance of getting through to the second round runoff of the Presidential election, let alone winning.[2] The whole purpose of having a Green candidate was to maximize first-round ballots as a vital signal to everyone of the Greens' strength. This was important to deepen the credibility of Green politics, make the Greens more desirable as potential governmental coalition partners (which they had been since 1997), and allow them greater clout within any future government.

Lipietz did not help his cause on the campaign trail. He had a tendency to come across as overly sure of himself, in particular about some issues where a more seasoned

candidate would have been cautious. His first real gaffe
did him in, however. In an atmosphere in which France's
perennial Corsican independence problems were on elite
minds, he spoke carelessly about a future amnesty for
Corsican nationalists. The press then misquoted him as
favoring the amnesty of Corsican autonomist terrorists,
including one responsible for the recent murder of the
island's French Prefect. This set off a media feeding
frenzy.

Lipietz soldiered on, trying to get his campaign message
across. The three principal environmental planks of
his program were struggle against climate change
due to greenhouse gases, in particular by promoting
public transportation, "denuclearizing" French electricity
production (no small matter, since most of French
electricity is both from nuclear and cheap) and for a
return to a more ecologically sound system of food
production (indelicately put as "returning to a peasant
France" in order to court the followers of José Bové).
Beyond environmentalism proper, the campaign took a
series of strong Leftish reform positions in favor
of lowering the working week below 35 hours,
increasing the availability of child care, establishing
voting rights for immigrants, re-introducing proportional
representation, regularizing the legal status of illegal
immigrants, and reforming pensions without challenging
the fundamentally public status of French social security.
Nothing worked to pry the media off Lipietz and Corsica.
Lipietz's opinion poll ratings went down like a stone, a
very serious matter for everyone on the French Left since
the Left's final Presidential candidate, Socialist Prime
Minister Lionel Jospin, would need every vote that he
could scrape up to defeat incumbent President Jacques
Chirac in the Presidential runoff. The last straw was an

article in *Le Monde*, France's newspaper of record (close to the Socialists and not above getting mixed up in the intricacies of Presidential politics despite its serious tone) that claimed that Lipietz had actually helped the FNLC (the Corsican National Liberation Front) write its program. Lipietz denied this, but the damage was huge nonetheless. Lipietz's campaign director eventually resigned, leaving his candidate swinging in winds of controversy. Finally, the Greens, prompted by elements in the party that had never accepted the Lipietz candidacy in the first place, decided to cut their losses by calling another national convention in early October to name a new candidate. Lipietz then got fired, and Noel Mamère, the centrist whom he had defeated in June, was nominated to succeed him.

There were underlying reasons why something like this soap opera was almost bound to occur. The French public and electorate naturally divide into multiple partisan allegiances on either side of a general Left-Right line. The names and numbers of the different players have changed over time, but the game has remained constant, as France's history demonstrates. To take only the twentieth century, for example, there has always been some sort of extreme Left "revolutionary" grouping, sometimes several[3]. The Center Left has been occupied by Socialists and "Radicals" (who were in fact liberals). The Right has mirrored the Left, with its own anti-democratic extreme at the far end of the spectrum, from Royalists to Fascists earlier to today's racist anti-immigrant *Front National*. In recent times, the Center Right has been a complicated mix of Christian Democrats, Liberals and Gaullists.

Charles de Gaulle, the towering figure of modern French politics, once allowed that a "country with 300 varieties of cheese" was likely to be nearly ungovernable. Of course all democratic polities are complex amalgamations of the wide range of citizen preferences that modern societies produce. Two-party systems promote the aggregation of interests from diverse parts of the population into two broad, more or less coherent, coalitions. In multi-party polities this work of aggregation has to be done in different ways. The French propensity for changing constitutions—Five Republics (and upwards of a score of constitutions) in all since 1789, two since 1945—demonstrates that satisfactory solutions have not always been easy to find.

What needs to happen is translation from a multiparty populace and electorate into viable coalitions for governance. The ways for doing this in the Fifth Republic (since 1958) are largely contained in electoral laws. Legislative and Presidential elections thus start out with a first multiparty round of voting, then followed by a winner-take-all second poll that is usually a runoff between the two best-placed candidates from the first round.[4] The system is designed to allow voters to express their particular preferences in the first round and oblige them to transfer their votes to one of two available alternatives, usually the larger parties of the Left and Right, in the runoff. It is also meant to encourage coalitional practices among parties, since coalitions provide the route to political power.

For smaller groups this obliges difficult choices. In first rounds of voting, the goal must be to present a strong and coherent picture of party identity, accentuating difference from the others. For the runoff, however, the party usually has to encourage its first round supporters to back another group with a different identity. Moreover, for small parties the only route to power is through coalitional deals with larger parties, which enjoins a certain moderation of identity. Figuring out how to navigate this is not easy, since small parties want to be as strong as possible to oblige larger parties to include some of their positions in ultimate coalitional compromise.

The system has been particularly vexing for the Greens. They were latecomers to the French political scene, making their first electoral breakthroughs only in 1989, rapidly becoming significant enough to join the Socialists, Communists and Left Radicals in the "Plural Left" governmental coalition around Lionel Jospin in 1997. Green politics in France, as in the rest of Europe, began as a "movement" mobilizing around environmental issues, not a party. Since environmental questions are not usually either Left or Right, the movement attracted interest and support from across the French spectrum. When the choice was made to become a party, internal factionalism, always prominent in French politics, intensified. This is easy to understand. Being a social movement usually means foregrounding specific issues, environmentalism in the Greens' case. Being a serious player in party politics means having to take positions on the whole range of issues that ordinary politics covers. The environmental movement's original cause thus had to be "hyphenated" to positions on managing the economy, international affairs, taxation, jurisprudence, the European Union, and defense policy, to mention only the most important. The problem is that there are as many ways to work this hyphenation as there are partisan approaches.

The troubled recent history of French environmental politics attests to the chronic nature of these problems. The Greens took off in the late 1980s, moving from but 4% of the vote in the 1988 Presidential election to 11% in the 1989 elections to the European Parliament (held under proportional representation rules), 15% at the 1992 regional elections and 12% in the 1993 legislative elections. Almost as quickly as the Greens took off, however, they began to decline—to 6% in the 1994 European elections. Perplexed, when the time came to designate candidates for the 1995 Presidential election, environmentalist leaders went in all directions. Dominique Voynet, the official Green candidate, ran a campaign that "hyphenated" environmentalism with Leftish reformism (somewhat like Lipietz's approach). Brice Lalonde, another leader, ended up backing a Right-Wing candidate. Antoine Waechter, one of the party's founders, made himself a candidate to publicize his position that environmentalism should not compromise with either the Left or the Right. Noel Mamère supported the Socialist candidate. Bad results were foreordained, therefore. Voynet got only 3.35% of the vote, slightly less than the 3.83% that Waechter had obtained in 1988.

In crisis, and anticipating the 1998 Legislative election (which was advanced to 1997 when President Chirac dissolved Parliament), the Green leaders decided to strike a deal with the Socialists, the Left's largest party, which gave them a small number of "winnable" seats where the Socialists agreed to stand down in exchange for Green stand-downs in a larger number of potentially winnable Socialist constituencies. The results were mixed. The Greens got a mere 4.5% of the vote overall in the constituencies where they stood (compared to the high point of 1993). Moreover, a wide range of different factions inside the party disapproved of the strategy the leadership had chosen. The party did win eight parliamentary seats, however, and then obtained the Ministry of the Environment (Voynet) in Jospin's new "plural Left" government. The hope, obviously, was that the new credibility from participation in the government and majority would pump up future support and unite the party. The first test of this was to be the 2002 Presidential campaign. Everyone knew that it would be a tough test, including the six official fractions inside the party Congress that met and squabbled in December 2000 to prepare the balloting in June 2001 that nominated Lipietz.

Lipietz was a leader in the Greens' left-most faction, as his *gauchisant*, '68er biography would have led one to anticipate. Since Lipietz's Leftism had been formed in struggles against the once hegemonic Communist party, this meant "hyphenating" environmental issues to "new Left" perspectives. These perspectives had their domestic dimensions such as deepening democratic participation in France, decentralization, redistributing resources to the poor, finding new ways to assimilate immigrants, restructuring work and employment policies. They also had important international dimensions that connected with many of the concerns of the powerful French anti-globalization movement, global environmentalism (Kyoto and more), world hunger and poverty issues, tied to international ecotaxes. [5]

Lipietz was a politician, and behind his program was a strategy for winning votes. In his eyes, the electoral decline of the Communist party and the Centrist dynamic of the Socialists opened up a swath of potential supporters who might be enticed to vote Green if the

Green campaign focused Leftwards. A priori, this was a serious position. Upwards of 15% of the electorate had been electorally "orphaned" by changes in the Left's former two large parties, underlined by the fact that early polls gave various Trotskyist candidates surprising support. Quite as important, Lipietz had quiet support inside the party from Dominique Voynet, who had herself campaigned "leftwards" in 1995 and who, rather more importantly, had political reasons to reduce the number of nominating votes for Noel Mamère. Mamère was a centrist whose electoral strategy aimed at attracting Centrist and Center Right voters with a different "hyphenation" of the environmentalist political project. Mamère was also close to the Socialist party leadership and its own Presidential election strategy.

It is not at all clear that Voynet actually wanted to see Lipietz nominated, but she did try to reduce Mamère's support prior to the nominating convention in June. This, together with the hard work that Lipietz himself had done, was what got Lipietz the nomination. The inside story thus meant that the Lipietz candidacy was in trouble immediately, well before his Corsican remarks. One would have been politically deaf not to hear the negative comments about Lipietz's Red+Green strategic line coming from the Socialist Party and from the pro-Socialist Mamère camp inside the Greens from the minute the nomination result was announced. In Lipietz's own words later, "the PS...[had]...a dilemma. It hoped for an environmentalist candidate to counter Corinne Lepage [on the Center Right] but not one who was either too Green or too strong. On the other hand, if the Green candidate is weakened, this poses a problem of reserve votes for Jospin..."[6] From the beginning Lipietz's campaign was thus a political accident waiting to happen.

The sooner he could be brought down, the better for the Socialists, a large number of Greens, the Center Right and, of course, corporate powers interested in minimizing Green influence and making the Greens look foolish. Lipietz's imprudent remarks on Corsica provided the pretext.

The deeper question must be to what extent this unpleasant episode reflects the contradictions of Green politics on the European continent more generally. France is an unusually complicated place because of the constant balancing act that all smaller parties must make between asserting sharp programmatic identities around environmental issues and more moderate self-presentation as potential allies of larger parties in ways that open paths to political power. This undoubtedly creates the kind of internal political life in parties like the Greens that Lipietz described after his downfall. The "factions (*courants* in the original...) which are supposed to structure internal debate, have become stables or clans whose chiefs negotiate with each other...and this has become tightly linked to the choice between movement and governing party. For a long time the Greens knew how to be...a party of struggle and government. Today certain leaders want to impose a different model, one of hyperrealism. It is in this sense that we should understand the slogan 'let us make the Greens into an adult party.' This means a professionalized party where the leaders do politics while everyone else brings them to power. From that point on what matters is maintaining oneself in institutions and, naturally, the question of alliances becomes crucial. It becomes indispensable to minimize what differentiates us from our allies in order to conserve positions of power."[7]

This is not a new understanding of the complexities of coalition politics in a democracy, but it is an accurate one. Movements are different from parties. Movements exist to change peoples' minds about particular issues, usually by mobilization on the political system from "outside." Parties, in contrast, exist to win a piece of the governmental action. When movements become parties they tempt fate, therefore, because they will inevitably have to face new issues about compromise to gain influence in the political system. This is not to say that it is inconceivable that movement-like parties or party-like movements cannot exist, even succeed. It is to say, however, that building and sustaining the complex coexistence of objectives that they need is very difficult. Lipietz's point of view on this represents one pole. "We, the Greens, represent a new and different social project, one which is not yet shared by the majority. Through social mobilization, working with associations, unions… our goal is to lead people to change their mentalities. Strengthened by this, we'll be able to get concessions from our alliance partners that are based on acceptable compromises. Participation in the institutions does not take precedence over everything else. You cannot make society change by decree."[8] On the other pole are those who think that they can make a difference by being present in places where power is exercised, who feel that the issues are too urgent now to proceed differently and who claim that the only way of strengthening the movement side of party life is by obtaining the resources that only participating in power can endow. Alain Lipietz's difficult summer illustrates what can happen when Greens split the differences badly.

Endnotes

[1]Rather than engage in lengthy footnoting here, I would suggest that curious readers consult Lipietz's website, lipietz.net and that of the French Greens, www.les-verts.org

[2]France's President is elected in two rounds. In the first anyone with sufficient public presence to pass the eligibility criterion of a petition signed by 500 signatures of elected officials (and France has many thousands of these) can run, which means that every shape and size of political group, from Trotskyists to hunters and fishermen, puts someone up. In the second round the two candidates with the largest number of first round votes face off.

[3]For the longest period this was composed of a large Communist party (which regularly won 20%+ of the vote), loyal to the Soviet Union, itself surrounded by grouplets of anti-communist revolutionaries (Lipietz originated politically in one of these). More recently the Communists have declined, leaving larger space for other claimants.

[4]This is not the whole story. Some elections, like those to the European Parliament, are based on proportional representation.

[5]ATTAC, France's main anti-globalization movement, has been an extraordinary domestic success and, in part through the wide and multilingual circulation of le Monde Diplomatique, whose editors are active in the movement, internationally. ATTAC chapters now exist across the world and have been the major forces behind things like the Porto Alegre "anti-summits."

[6]Interview in *Marianne*, 29 October 2001 (translation GR).

[7]Lipietz interview in *Marianne*, op cit

[8]Ibid.

The Evolution of Greens in Europe

Arnold Cassola

The Greens in Europe now have over twenty years of parliamentary experience and more than six years of experience of being in governing coalitions. Such an evolution of the political role of the Greens has meant an evolution of the Greens as a party on three different levels: at the level of national governments; at the European Party level, and at the level of the European Parliament.

The evolution of Green politics over the years has been reflected in various ways. It was during the 1980s that the national Green Parties in Europe felt the need to establish a wider European Network. The result of this was the establishment of the *Coordination of European Green Parties* in 1984. This coordination started building the Green family on a European basis, but did not have any political mandate at all. It was more concentrated on networking amongst the different Green Parties in Europe.

At the beginning of the 1990s, when the Coordination had increased to more than twenty members, the necessity to have a *European Greens* organization that was also a politically mandated body became apparent. This led to the founding of the European Federation of Green Parties (EFGP) in Majvik, Finland in June 1993. There were twenty-three founding members, and these included Green Parties from the European Union, Green Parties from EU applicant countries (like Hungary and Malta) and Green Parties from other parts of the European continent (such as Georgia, Switzerland, and Norway). The founding fathers and mothers of the EFGP had a real vision: In fact, the EFGP is the only European political organization to have had as full founding members both Green Parties from within and from outside of the European Union.

Today, the EFGP is made up of 32 full member parties and five observers. The Federation's political structures are made up of the Congress, which meets every three years and which is made up of around 400 delegates; the Council, which meets twice a year and comprises a total of approximately 65 delegates, and the nine member Committee, which is elected for a period of three years.

In its nine years of existence, the EFGP has developed regional networks, which meet a number of times during the year to discuss problems of regional interest. The major regional networks of the federation are: The Green East-West Dialogue, the Mediterranean Network, the Baltic Green Network, the North Sea Greens, and the Alpine Greens.

When the Federation was first founded in 1993, there were Greens in parliament, but Greens were not in government. Since then, much water has passed under the bridge. In fact, from 1995 on, Greens have been a part of various national coalition governments, including those in Finland, Italy, Georgia, Slovakia, Germany, France, Belgium and the Ukraine. Moreover, today the Greens can boast of nearly 200 parliamentarians in National Parliaments in 16 European countries. The EFGP has evolved significantly since its foundation. While still working hard on networking among different parties and other Green actors, it does substantial work on political issues in collaboration with the national parties and with the Greens in the European Parliament.

The Nice Treaty of the European Union, which was drawn up in the French Riviera city in December 2000, foresees the formal recognition of European political parties with proper statutes and financial rules. In the future, therefore, the European Greens should be playing an even more important political role, not only because they will get direct funding from the European Commission, but mainly because a more integrated European Union will favor the discussion and development of politics at the supranational level.

Finally, the EFGP has played a leading role, together with the Green Federations of Africa, the Americas and Asia/Pacific, in the organization of the Canberra Global Greens Meeting (April 2001) and in the creation of the *Global Greens Charter.*

The development of Green politics and the growing strength of the Greens from the 1980s onwards has also brought about a change in the structure of Green power in the European parliament. The European parliament, which is based in Strasbourg and Brussels, has been elected directly by the people since 1979. In the first year the Greens did not win a single parliamentary seat. This result reflected the lack of strength of the Greens in Europe. In 1984, the first Greens were elected to the European Parliament, showing that the Greens had increased their following during the previous five years. However, the number of Green Members of the European Parliament (MEPs) was still too small for them to form an autonomous parliamentary group. The Greens therefore joined forces with other smaller groups, like the Radicals, to form what was called the *Rainbow Group.*

The 1989 European parliamentary elections brought about a significant change, in that for the first time the Greens were strong enough to form their own autonomous parliamentary group. Made up of a total of 27 Green MEPs, it became a strong little political force that started making people look up and take notice. The Greens in the European Parliament concentrated on the following priorities during the period from 1989 to 1994: the internal market, institutional issues, regional eco-development, nuclear power, agriculture, North-South solidarity, fundamental rights and liberties, and the fight against social exclusion of the weaker strata of society.

The 1994 European parliamentary elections witnessed a confirmation of the Green potential. The Greens increased their number by one, thus forming a 28 member group for the 1994-1999 legislature. The strongest national group this time was made up of the German contingent (the French had been the strongest national group in 1989-1994). During the 1994-1999 parliamentary term, the Greens witnessed an enormous increase in their ratings amongst the various European populations. One Green Party after another, the Finnish, the Italians, the French, and the Germans started being entrusted with governmental responsibilities. European citizens began to understand that environmentalism was not to be viewed in a vacuum, but rather as an issue to be dealt with in relation to many others. It began to become clear that the environment was closely related to various other important issues that condition the everyday quality of life, such as transport issues, energy production, health issues, and food safety. The more people started realizing this, the more they began to vote for the Greens.

The 1999 European elections proved to be a veritable bonanza of votes for the Greens. The Greens elected 38 Members to the European parliament, joined forces with a small regionalist group, and thus gave birth to the fourth biggest formation in the European Parliament, the *Green-EFA Group*, which today numbers 45 MEPs. The three strongest groups in the EP are the European Popular Party (Christian Democrats), the Party of European Socialists, and the Party of European Liberals.

The importance of the present green-EFA Group in the European Parliament is paramount. In fact, the Greens can sway the vote from the Christian Democratic majority if they join forces with the Socialists and Liberals. On the other hand, they can also sway the vote if they ally themselves with the Christian Democrats, as happened, for example, on the issue of cloning, when Britain was condemned for its cloning policies. Of course, in a case like this, the reasons behind the vote of the Christian democrats and those of the Greens could be very different. Regardless, the fact remains that the 45 strong Green formations can make a difference.

The importance of the Greens has also been reflected in the Presidencies of the various parliamentary committees. In fact, at the present moment, the Greens hold, amongst others, the Presidency of the Social Affairs Committee, the first Vice Presidency of the Agricultural Committee and the Vice Presidency of the Environmental Committee; that is, three of the most important topics today in the European Union and in the EU candidate countries.

One issue that came up in the course of the International Conference on Green Politics at Brandeis is *compromise*, with a negative connotation attached to it. It would seem that arriving at a middle of the road agreement in politics is a negative thing. However, politics is the art of the possible. The Green political experience in Europe has shown that until Greens were in opposition, they were really free to protest strongly against all things they disagreed with. However, cry as they might, they were unable to influence the political agenda in the direction they would have liked. Greens in opposition and, even worse, outside parliament, clamored for 100 percent and got zero.

From within government Greens have managed to influence the political agenda and to bring about important changes. Of course, being in a coalition, and the minority partner at that, means that Greens in government can never obtain the 100 percent they would like to have. At the end, after some tough dealing, we could end up with obtaining 20 percent of what we originally wanted. It is necessary to ask: what is better? Staying in the opposition asking for the maximum and never getting anything? Or being in government, asking for the maximum and ending up getting one fifth of one's goal? To me the second option is the better one.

Some practical examples demonstrate the benefits of compromise: In Germany, the Greens in government did not get the desired speed in the phasing out of nuclear energy, but they did manage to start off the process. And the generation of Germans born today will be able to see their country free of nuclear energy before they reach the age of thirty! Just imagine if the Greens had not been in government. The process would not have been started at all. Look at Belgium: In January of 2000, a naturalization and citizenship law was drawn up for the many people from outside the EU who had been working illegally in Belgium for years. Of course, it is not the ideal hundred percent liberal immigration law that the Belgian Greens wanted; however, the law was drawn up because the Greens were in government. Today, there is a legal framework for immigration, which undoubtedly can be improved, but which would not have existed at all had the Greens not been in power.

If the Greens want radical changes and want to be influential and instrumental in bringing them about, then Greens have also got to change themselves and evolve. When Green power became so strong that we could no longer be kept out of government, the following logic seemed to prevail in the establishment: Greens have proven that they are the experts in the environmental field. So we entrust them with the ministry of the environment. And the first ministries the Greens were put in charge of in Finland, in Italy, in France were indeed the environmental ministries. The underlying message was that the Greens should be responsible for the environment, and for the environment only! The Greens did not understand anything about anything else! Well, time has proven that this is not so. Environmental issues are interconnected. The increase in respiratory diseases as a result of increased and badly managed traffic, the pollution caused by energy plants based on fossil fuels, food safety crises, such as the 'chicken dioxin' in Belgium, 'foot and mouth' in Britain and 'Mad Cow disease' all over Europe, and the unknown effects on health of genetically modified organisms have all contributed to raising the profile of the Greens, to highlighting their foresight and professional knowledge on these subjects.

From the original 1995 restricted environmental portfolios, the Greens have moved on to hold various other ministries, such as Equal Opportunities, Agriculture and Forestry in Italy, Health and Social Services in Finland, a Solidary Economy in France, Health, Agriculture, Food Safety and Consumer Protection and Foreign Affairs in Germany, Mobility and Transport, Health, Environment and Consumer Affairs, Development Cooperation and Energy and Sustainable Development in Belgium. At the beginning of the 21st century it has become amply clear to all that the Greens in Europe had evolved from a one issue environmental party into a multi issue party that has as its top priorities on its political agenda the environment, the social dimension and the respect of democracy and basic human rights.

Hopefully, following these first years of governmental experience, Greens in government are here to stay. However, some lessons can already be learned from our past experience, and it is good for all those Green Parties who are faced with the prospect of forming part of a coalition government to keep this in mind (the Irish Greens and the Dutch Greens might have to face this decision in 2002).

A first recommendation is: If a Green Party enters government, it has to ensure that the Party remains strong. It is very important that alongside strong Green ministers there is also a strong Green Party leadership that can still stand for the demands of the grass roots environmental movements.

The second recommendation is that the Greens in government should ensure for themselves a strong political visibility, in order not to be swallowed up by the major components of the coalition.

In the third place, it is desirable that Greens enter government when their strength is an essential one for the coalition to survive and thrive. This will make the Greens more relevant to the political agenda, to its coalition party, and for the public.

Fourth, it is very important to have a well-written autonomous electoral program to show clearly what the Greens will stand for when in government, beyond the environment. Obviously, it remains clear that in a government coalition Greens can only accomplish part of their electoral program.

Finally, it is of paramount importance that Greens bargain well *before* the elections, and have the approved government coalition program published and well publicized amongst the electorate once this has been decided.

The Greens in Europe have come a long way. Certainly we must not rest on our laurels. There is still a long way to go before we reach our objectives for the betterment of the quality of life for people and for an equitable distribution of resources on this planet. After having developed from a mainly environmentalist party into one that can manage transport, energy, social and democracy issucs, it is now probably time to go a step forward. While never renouncing our original environmentalist and pacifist origins, and while giving a priority to the less fortunate sectors of society, we should also start contributing to the formulation of Green policies on education, health and economy, since these areas are of fundamental importance to all citizens today.

II. Green Politics in the United States

Running for President on the Green Party Ticket: Barriers to Third Party Entry

Theresa Amato and Ralph Nader˙

Article II of the U.S. Constitution, the part where it says, "No person except a natural born citizen, or a citizen of the United States, at the time of the adoption of this Constitution, shall be eligible to the office of President." is disconnected from *realpolitik*. If it reflected today's reality, it would read more along these lines:

No person who cannot overcome arcane ballot access laws in 50 states and is not a billionaire shall be eligible to the office of president except those nominated by the reigning duopoly and condoned by the *New York Times* and *Washington Post* or the five polling companies that are contracted to provide polls to bipartisan, corporate-funded commissions on presidential debates lest they be thought to clutter the playing field or deprive one of the other candidates of their rightful entitlement to all the votes that the aspiring person might otherwise take.

Running for president as a third-party candidate permits an eyewitness view of the multifaceted barriers that prevent third parties in this country from competing fairly in the democratic process. The hurdles are so prevalent that leaders of the oligarchic regimes in foreign countries might blush. From media coverage to ballot access and participation in the presidential debates, the obstacles to competing in the political process loom large and the political will to reduce them is puny.

46

Our campaign was launched in February 2000 to seek the presidential nomination of the Green Party because of the democracy gap in our country. The announcement came at an opening address at the Madison Hotel in Washington, D.C., replete with an extensive explanation about how civil society is having a harder time getting things done because corporate influence and dollars have rendered a bought-and-paid-for political scene in Washington that either is beholden to their corporate paymasters or largely indifferent to corporate control of some of our basic public institutions. The resulting loss attributable to this gap was discussed in detail. The *Washington Post*, which is headquartered across 15th Street, could not be bothered to send a reporter. There were some cameras and other reporters, but almost no coverage. The announcement earned a 300-word squib in the *New York Times*, akin to the amount of space they devote to a couple of marriage notices.

The first lesson of entering the race for president as a citizen seeking a third-party nomination rather than as a major party candidate was that one can count on receiving almost no media coverage. If you don't speak eight-second sound bites, you're not likely to get coverage in the standard 17 minutes of corporate news cycles exclusively fuelled by leads that bleed, lengthy weather reports, cute animal stories, and chitchat between the anchors. Even when the campaign filled Madison Square Garden in mid-October, on 10 days notice, with more than 15,000 paying people, the *Washington Post* still did not cover it. The Nader campaign was unique in its ability to draw such large paying crowds to its political rallies. It is one thing to fail to provide daily coverage of third-party candidates, but it is another matter to fail to report the history-making aspects of a third-party campaign.

Throughout the campaign, all that the press wanted to cover was the horse race. A candidate can talk about the death penalty; child poverty; racial profiling; corporate crime, fraud, and abuse; the failed war on drugs; the millions of people without health insurance; campaign finance failures; and all the pressing problems of the day. The candidate can go to all fifty states, to housing projects and homeless shelters, and put out sixty-plus position papers, and two to four press releases a day. Yet at the end of the day, the only thing the press cares about is the horse race and whether a third-party candidate is "stealing" votes from either or both of the two-party mind-set: a candidate who competes in a primary is accorded equal footing as a "challenger" with the "frontrunner," while a third-party candidate who competes in the general election is considered a "spoiler" for daring to enter the duopolists' playing field and stealing votes.

If you do get coverage as third-party candidate, it is likely to be cast as some kind of style or feature story. Third-party candidates are not news; they are treated as oddities-or worse, clutter. The *New York Times*, as early as June, pronounced in its lead editorial that the voters should have a clear thumbs up or thumbs down choice on just Bush or Gore. The Nader-LaDuke campaign was considered to be cluttering the field. Over the course of the campaign, it became apparent that the *New York Times* would say just about anything to make sure that Al Gore won. This was the case not only for the editorial board, since some reporters would editorialize as well. There were some notable exceptions among the media, such as *The Village Voice* and *The Nation*, but not many.

Of course, most third parties cannot afford much media advertising. Our campaign spent under $2 million on media advertising. Pat Buchanan spent nearly everything from the Reform Party millions on ballot access or advertisements. According to posted FEC records, the Bush campaign spent approximately $73 million on media. The Gore campaign spent approximately $51 million. This does not include what the parties or advocacy groups spent on media on behalf of the major-party candidates. A substantial percentage of the contributions made to campaigns or parties are thus funneled into the television broadcasters' pockets to pay for ads that are mostly displayed in the swing states, with virtually all other states being ignored.

The Alliance for Better Campaigns, a public-interest group led by Paul Taylor, has a study on its Website (www.bettercampaigns.org) about the broadcasters and their price gouging entitled "Gouging Democracy." (See also www.Greedytv.org, and Matt Farray's article in the Summer 2001 issue of the *National Civic Review*) The television industry raked in more than $770 million for political ads in the 2000 elections; of the stations surveyed, most provided less than 45 seconds a night of coverage—*total*—for the candidates. No wonder the television networks barely cover the two major party conventions. It appears to be better for their bottom line to freeze out the politicians and make them pay top dollar for ads in order to get any time at all on publicly owned airwaves.

Of course, since the system serves the duopolists well, neither party in Congress has much incentive to change it. Candidates seem to prefer having controlled messages compacted into 30-second ads. (Some candidates refused to have a press conference for weeks on end!) If we want fair elections, though, then the landlords of the airwaves—the taxpayers who own this piece of the commonwealth—should be able to require that the tenants (the broadcasters who rent these public assets) provide free airtime to candidates who are on the ballot for public office.

Apart from the problems in getting coverage, how do candidates for president actually get in the position where the voters can vote for them? In the United States, each state has not only its own specially designed (butterfly) ballot but also its own arcane set of grossly complicated procedures for getting on the ballot. Mind you, bipartisan-controlled state assemblies created all these incredible obstacles.

Richard Winger, who publishes *Ballot Access News* (www.ballot-access.org), does a formidable job of chronicling these outrages. Among the crippling provisions encountered during election 2000, consider these:

• To qualify for the ballot in Texas, a political party needed to collect 37,713 signatures in a 75-day period; those who signed the petition could not have voted in the state's primary.

• In North Carolina, a party needed 51,324 signatures by May 15 of the election year. By statute, the petition has a must-carry phrase that reads, "The signers of this petition intend to organize a new political party..." To contemplate the chilling effect, simply ask yourself: When was the last time you signed something that would require you to commit to organizing a new political party?

- In Virginia, a candidate needs 10,000 signatures, four hundred from each congressional district. Circulators can only petition in the county they live in and an adjacent county.

- In Illinois, a new party needs 25,000 signatures to get on the ballot, while "established parties" only need 5,000 signatures.

- In Oklahoma, 36,202 signatures are required for a candidate to qualify for the ballot. With a population of 3,350,000, Oklahoma ranks 28 in the nation in population, but its total signature requirement is the fourth highest in the United Sates and highest per capita in the country.

- Oklahoma (along with South Dakota) doesn't allow write-in votes, which strikes us as a lawsuit waiting to happen.

Those are just the raw number barriers. But there are also excessive filing fees, early deadlines, and administrative hurdles. For example, in Pennsylvania, the state requires signature forms on special colored paper; it only provided four hundred forms though our volunteers needed more than two thousand. The state would not accept forms downloaded from the Internet. In West Virginia and Georgia, the filing fee is $4,000! In Michigan, petition forms had to be on odd-sized paper (8-$\frac{1}{2}$ by 13 inches).

In many states, our petitioners were harassed and threatened with arrest by officials with a shallow understanding of the First Amendment for circulating petitions in public places or taxpayer-financed parks and recreation areas. In Mississippi, the mayor of Tupelo stopped our petitioners from working the town square at a festival on the Fourth of July. In Ohio, our petitioners were stopped from collecting signatures at a public market in West Cleveland. The reports from our volunteer petitioners were profiles in courage.

Of course, the Green Party is not the only one to face this challenge. The Libertarian Party, the Reform Party, the Natural Law Party, and the Constitutional Party... all of the third parties have to go through this charade every time they seek to compete with the established duopolists. What happens when progress is made? The Democrats and Republicans who control the state assemblies and legislatures just run back into session to make the hurdles tougher.

For these reasons, we need to encourage adoption of a model ballot law and remove barriers to entry. The Appleseed Center for Electoral Reform and the Harvard Legislative Research Bureau set forth a Model Act for the Democratization of Ballot Access[1] that include these reforms:

• Lower signature thresholds to a reasonable level

• Eliminate outrageous filing fees

• End constraints on the identity of petitioners and signers

• Establish a filing deadline of, and allow corrections until, September 1 of election year

• Use random sampling for verification

- Eliminate so-called sore-loser bans

- Accept all write-in candidates

- Apply all reforms to independent candidates

- Allow performance in the last two elections as qualification

- Optimally, use a threshold of 0.05 percent party registration to determine ballot access

We also suggest these additional voting reforms to engage more voters in the process:

- Adopt same-day voter registration. Just when most people get excited about politics, in the last few weeks before the election, it is too late to register in most states. State and local officials should act to follow the lead of those six states that allow eligible voters to register right up to the election.

- Open up the two-party system by adopting proportional representation. Around the world, multiparty systems of proportional representation allow citizens more-direct representation in their government. Municipalities across the nation—including New York City—used proportional representation systems for years before the major parties crushed the system. There are countless opportunities at the state and local levels to reestablish this markedly more democratic system.

• Gauge public opinion at the polls by initiating a national nonbinding advisory referendum. We should put forth nonbinding referenda on salient local, state, and national issues for voting on Election Day. This would allow the public an additional mechanism to directly instruct their representatives- instead of forcing elected officials to rely on questionable commercial polls.

• Make every vote count by allowing instant runoff voting. At every government level, we should follow the lead of London and the countries of Ireland and Australia and establish a system of instant runoff voting. By allowing voters to rank candidates (see articles in the Summer 2001 issue of the *National Civic Review* by Castillo and McGrath, and Ritchie and Hill, for an explanation of how this works), we can liberate citizens to choose their favorite candidates, and ignore the cries of "wasted vote" and "spoiler."

• Adopt a binding, non-of-the-above option. Voters should be able to reject unsatisfactory candidates by choosing none of the above and, if NOTA wins, force a new election with new candidates.

• Demand strict enforcement of the Voting Rights Act. The debacle in Florida highlighted the extreme need for reassessing the impact of race and class on electoral mechanics. The VRA must be enforced strictly to safeguard the basic rights of citizens across the nation.

• Accept a standardized national ballot. There would have been no butterfly-ballot controversy if state and local officials had cooperated in creating an effective standardized system for national elections.

• Make election officials nonpartisan (not bipartisan) at the local, state, and national levels. Officials usually respect the notion that democracy trumps party loyalty, but inherent in a party system is the danger that a few partisan officials will tilt the process in practice. State and local officials must establish systems by which nonpartisan officials control the all-important mechanics of election.

• Count write-in ballots in all states.

• Provide public disclosure of vote totals by precinct on the Internet.

• Provide access to voter registration forms on the Internet.

• Provide voter pamphlets online, at polling places, and by mail to voters.

• Provide nonpolitical assignment of ballot lines.

If a third-party candidate braves the Sisyphean daily task of getting a message out to the voters when almost no one in the corporate-conglomerated fourth estate is willing to provide coverage, and if the candidate spends tens of thousands of hours and dollars (in some cases millions) to overcome the ballot access hurdles, there still remains the biggest barrier of all, the traditional mechanism of reaching tens of millions of people in the age of television: participation in presidential debates. The term *presidential debate* is almost a quaint misnomer considering the love fest of agreement and the exercise of diversion displayed between the major-party candidates during those encounters held last fall. The gatekeeper for the viewing voters is a little-known entity called the Commission on Presidential Debates (CPD).

In 1907, Congress enacted the Tillman Act, prohibiting corporate contributions to any candidate running for federal office. In the early 1970s, Congress enacted the Federal Election Campaign Act (FECA), which, in part, created an administrative agency, the Federal Election Commission (FEC), to enforce the act's campaign finance and disclosure laws, which include the 1907 prohibition of corporate contributions to federal campaigns. Under these laws, for-profit corporations are not allowed to spend money "in connection with" campaigns for federal office, unless the money is used for "nonpartisan activity."

Pursuant to the FECA, which should really be renamed the Duopoly Protection Act; the FEC in the late 1970s told the League of Women Voters (who used to sponsor the presidential debates) that they could not accept money from corporations to help defray the cost of debates.

In 1987, the Democratic and Republican Parties decided to take over the sponsorship of the debates by creating their own commission. Notably, the CPD is run by the former chairmen of the Democratic and Republican parties. After the CPD was established, the FEC (whose commission is composed of three Democrats and three Republicans) rejected its own general council's opinion, reversed its prior position, and adopted a regulation that allows corporations to spend money to help stage federal candidate debates.

This loophole created in the regulatory framework established by Congress allows corporate money to tilt the electoral playing field for the two major party candidates. It is our position that the FEC regulation exceeds the statutory authority granted by Congress and should be struck down. The National Voting Rights Institute and pro bono lawyers are currently asking the U.S. Supreme Court to consider the legality of this regulation.

If this legal challenge is successful, corporate sponsors of the CPD debates — which include beer and tobacco companies — would again be subject to the FECA's corporate contribution prohibition. We would then have presidential debates that do not look like Bud bowls filled with corporate logos and an Anheuser-Busch beer tent. In the age of the Invesco Stadium, the Fleet Center, the Target Center, the United Center, and other exercises in corporate naming, can we still imagine any sort of competition not replete with corporate advertisements even when the point is to elect the president of the United States?

Adding insult to injury, eligibility for getting a message out entails permission from a bipartisan commission, funded by beer and tobacco money, that sets an arbitrary standard of reaching a 15 percent rating in five polls of the commission's choosing- polls whose major media parent companies have executives who give lots of money to the duopolists. With these criteria, Abraham Lincoln would have been excluded from the debates; he wasn't even on the ballot in nine states. The debate commission made a mistake, from their viewpoint, by letting Ross Perot into the debates in 1992. The viewership shot up to more than ninety million Americans, and Perot got 19 percent of the vote. But four years later, after the Clinton and Dole camps decided to exclude Perot, network viewship plummeted to 42 million.

Another independent candidate, Jesse Ventura, got into the gubernatorial debates in Minnesota in 1998, and he became the governor. It was clear during the 2000 presidential election that the Republicans and the Democrats were not prepared to make this mistake again. We received a polite letter saying we didn't meet their self-serving criteria for participation. Who knew that the gatekeepers to the American presidency's electorate sit in a private office in Washington, D.C.?

Indeed, the commission was so terrified of competition they would not even let Ralph Nader physically near the debates. In October 2000, for the first debate at the University of Massachusetts, he had a ticket to get into the auditorium adjacent to the scene of the debates, but the CPD decided to use the state troopers to keep him from listening to the debate and talking to the media at the media trailer—despite the fact that the media had invited him to do so. There are countries abroad that we criticize for this kind of authoritarian behavior. We filed a lawsuit in connection with this action; the federal judge in Boston hearing the case denied the CPD's motion to dismiss.

No coverage, awful ballot laws, no access to the voters through debates...in the economic world, we would call each of these a barrier to entry that distorts the market from perfect competition. Imagine if we told entrepreneurs that before they were allowed to compete they had to have a 15 percent market share. You can be sure that there would be antitrust suits.

Between the ballot access hurdles and the debate commission, Nader 2000 brought eleven lawsuits in a nine-month campaign thanks to the help of the Brennan Center for Justice at the NYU Law School, the National Voting Rights Institute, and pro bono law firms. We had to arrange for the equivalent of a full-time public-interest law firm just to level the playing field to compete.

This does not even count the need to defend. In a striking case of corporate immolation worthy of a case study at the Harvard Business School, MasterCard decided to sue us for daring to parody their "Priceless" ad campaign in noncommercial use of our campaign finance spoof on the "things money can't buy"—a spot designed to move poll numbers and get Nader into the debates. Apparently, MasterCard doesn't share our sense of humor, and although they lost their attempt at a temporary restraining order, they are continuing to sue us even after the election for alleged copyright and trademark infringement.

Campaigns, of course, are not priceless. More than a half a billion dollars was raised in soft money by parties in the last election cycle. The *Washington Post* in February 2001 editorialized that "the campaign finance system is totally out of control... In each of the last two presidential cycles, the amount [of soft money] has doubled...If officeholders aren't being bought by such sums, the offices themselves surely are."[2]

The biggest obstacle to just government action is the corruption of our election campaigns by special-interest money. No one should have to sell out to big business or big donors to run a competitive campaign. Political campaigns should be publicly financed, just like public libraries, parks, and schools. We started the campaign with a $40,000 personal contribution by the candidate. Our average donation was less than $100. We raised a little over $8 million in nine months, taking no corporate money, no PAC money, and no soft money, and we did our frugal best to run a nationwide campaign with the energy of volunteers and the Green Party. To put it into perspective, the Democratic Party spent $8 million advertising in the state of Michigan alone.

To remove barriers to entry for third parties, we need to end legalized bribery and support publicly financed campaigns. The McCain-Feingold Bill that is pending as this article was written is not the solution to dirty-money politics. Although it eliminates soft money, the bill raises the hard-money limits, does not provide free airtime for candidates, and does not establish public financing. Therefore, the barriers to entry for serious candidates will remain.

If a candidate overcomes all of these structural barriers, there still remain a host of other problems, such as the bias in favor of the two-party system that we are taught in school, straw polls that do not include any of the other parties (Libertarian Party, Reform Party, Constitution Party, Green Party), and the influence of parental voting patterns. Hereditary voting practices have made voting for a third party an extraordinary political act. Third parties are viewed as freak institutions because the United States doesn't have proportional representation or instant runoff voting as other countries do, and because people are generally unaware of how third parties have advanced justice in this country by raising such radical ideas as abolition of slavery, women's suffrage, the graduated income tax, and deficit reduction.

In the mid-19th century, it took just six years for the Republicans to replace the Whigs as an emerging major party. Given the structural hurdles in place favoring the Democratic and Republican parties, what would it take for a startup to replace either of these entrenched parties today?

What is the price we pay for our forgone democracy? What does it cost us in efforts not undertaken and social justice left unrealized? Currently in the United States, there are 38 million poor people, 20 percent of children live in deep poverty, 80 percent of workers have lost ground since 1973 (after adjusting for inflation), 46 million people are without health insurance, there is a record level of personal bankruptcy, and total consumer debt is more than $6 trillion.

Our country faces critical housing needs, crumbling public works, global warming, forest destruction, air and water pollution, rampant corporate fraud, and numerous public health problems, all against a backdrop of sprawl and gated communities, billions spent on campaigns, a burgeoning prison industry with more than two million people incarcerated, a failed war on drugs, more than one hundred million eligible voters who do not vote, and states that cannot even process the votes of those who do.

Our two-party political system is engaged in an unfair restraint of democratic participation. It is a duopoly that has erected barriers to political engagement and is restricting the exercise of democracy in our country. Our laws do not countenance such an illegitimate concentration of power in the economy. Do we hold our political and democratic values in lesser esteem?

Endnotes

[1] In the *Harvard Journal on Legislation*, Summer 1999, 36 (2), 451-478.
[2] *Washington Post* editorial, Feb. 19, 2001, p. A32.

Ralph Nader was the Green Party candidate for president in the 2000 election.

Theresa Amato was the campaign manager of the national Nader 2000 campaign.

*This article, by Theresa Amato and Ralph Nader, was originally published as "So You Want to Run for President? Ha! Barriers to Third Party Entry," in *National Civic Review*, copyright 2001, John Wiley & Sons, Inc.

Staying Green While Building the Green Party of the United States

Annie Goeke

From the early 1980s to the present day, the Green political movement in this country has grown into a truly viable and fast growing political party called the Green Party of the United States. During all this building, no matter what the challenges have been, the Greens have maintained their connection to environmental issues through their candidates and the national Green Party platform. Ecological perspective is a basic value for Greens and this consciousness has spread worldwide, shown by how this Green political movement has expanded into over 80 countries. The U.S. Greens have been very much part of this building of the Global Greens initiative.

Since the U.S. green movement's inception in the mid 1980s, starting with the Green Party Organizing Committee and the Green Committees of Correspondence, the Green Party has evolved and grown. There had been numerous environmental movements prior to the 1980s, but none built on an ecological consciousness like the Greens. Ecological consciousness goes beyond the environmental perspective and is a holistic understanding of our place as humans in relation to nature and other humans.

 The U.S. Green movement has met with some success as well as struggles caused, in part, by our undemocratic electoral process.

At some point, people desired to go further than grass roots activism. To walk the talk, we knew there had to be a political party in this country that would engage in the issues that we feel are important. We knew we had to learn how our government system worked so that we could change it for a "greener" agenda. There was a need for us to start getting political and put ourselves on the line by running a political candidate. Doing this gave us visibility as we accepted our participation in the political debates. This has been an important area for us to express our "green" values, ideas and issues. The main four values being—non-violence, ecological wisdom, grass roots democracy and social justice.

It has always been known that the Green Party in this country is a grass roots political movement. What is less known is the national organizing and building of this political party. Until 1991, the Green Party was a broad-based coalition of Greens at the local, state, and national level. From the early nineties, there was debate amongst members about how the unifying structure of the Green Party would be planned and implemented. It was not until 1996 that the foundation of the Green's first nationwide organizing effort was formed due to the presidential campaign when we ran Ralph Nader for the first time. This gave some Greens the necessary vision, experience, and energy to start to constructively build a national campaign and a national political party.

Immediately following the 1996 elections, the Association of State Green Parties was established to focus mainly on party building that set in motion a period of rapid growth for the Green movement. Starting with only nine members State Green Parties at the founding meeting in Middleburg, Virginia, in November 1996, we have grown to a membership of 34 State Green Parties with more in the process of affiliating.

Our major leap came when we entered into the 2000 presidential race with Ralph Nader and Winona La Duke running as our candidates. This campaign gave us the visibility we needed to seriously enter into American politics as a true third political party. We now have gained the position as the third largest political party in this country and managed, with the help of Ralph Nader and his campaign, to gain ballot access during the campaign in 45 states. This was an amazing achievement considering all the challenges, blocks, and the little funds with which we had to work. As a truly grass roots party, so much of what we accomplished came from the human capital available to us. Individuals across the country committed themselves in helping to build this very necessary alternative political party.

So why are we considered alternative and why have so many individuals felt committed to joining us? Perhaps it is because we became the party known for the slogans—People over Profits—People Interests not Corporate Interests—We are not for sale. Democrats and Republicans are indentured to the concentration of power and control of private and public wealth. While the Green Party aims to be a party of a different kind of politics, a political party that transforms the way politics is carried on and allows for true democracy to exist.

Out of this party building, we were able to present our national Green Party platform and a series of resolutions that established key areas of focus for our presidential candidate and all our other Green Party candidates.

The key areas that framed our platform were: electoral reform, economic justice, human rights, health care, and environmental sustainability.

Before we gained the status of a viable political force, many Americans thought of us as solely environmentalists. Our challenge was to show that even though environmental issues are very much a part of our roots, as is the peace issue, we address other issues that concern the people in this country such as economic and social justice. We knew the importance of our work was to educate the public on how these issues are interconnected. We had to break that image of being "tree huggers" and show that the Greens are capable of being elected public officials. We had to show that our concerns and knowledge went beyond environmental issues. We had to convince our local communities that we do have solutions and ways to create a healthier environment and develop a more sustainable and just community.

There are many examples of Green Party candidates, elected Green Party officials and even state Green Parties supporting and creating initiatives and policies to do with the environment while promoting other important issues.

We have established ourselves as a new breed of political candidates. Most Greens have had experience in some form of activism, have come out of the grass roots movement, and many have developed a broad knowledge of the issues. Most local green groups have built strong coalitions with both national and local environmental groups.

Here are a few examples of how we maintain our connection to environmental issues through our political campaigning or as elected officials.

I ran last year as Auditor General for Pennsylvania. The role of an Auditor General has to do with state taxes. I found a way to connect an important environmental issue to my campaign by making energy efficiency one of my top priorities. My campaign promoted an initiative to implement alternative clean energy usage on state buildings. It gave me the advantage of discussing Pennsylvania's detrimental environmental record and the responsibility of this state for global warming.

Also in Pennsylvania, Bill Belitskus ran for a congressional seat. His main platform had to do with the Allegheny Forest protection. Brian Laverty, who got reelected on November 6, 2001, was on the Board of the Pennsylvania Environmental Network. There are Greens in this country who are writing up new legislation, ordinances and policies — many to do with the environment. We are not only creating these new initiatives but publicizing them, getting support for them and implementing them.

In Santa Monica, California, well-known Green Mike Feinstein is mayor. Due to his position, he has found a way for the city of Santa Monica to accept a "green" building ordinance. This ordinance requires higher energy efficiency than that of the state requirement. It encourages the use of recycled building materials and the recycling of demolition materials. The city works with businesses, showing them how they can profit from this way of building. They even supply them with a CD-ROM on the various methods to make the building more energy efficient. This effectively shows how the environment and economics can go hand in hand.

Across the nation, many of the Green Party elected council members are involved in projects specifically to do with the halting of sprawl by working on infill projects that have to do with public transit and affordable housing at the same time. All are also working aggressively on spending money for parks and open space.

We are the only political party in the United States that expresses concerns about global issues and about how we affect other places in the world. An old slogan of ours has been " Think globally, Act locally." Many of us were the ones out on the streets in Seattle, Washington, D.C., Quebec and all the other places where mass action campaigns have been organized.

Over the years we have developed and strengthened our ties with other Green Parties and Greens from around the world. We have been an important contributor to the global Green movement and helped with organizing the Global Greens 2001 Conference in Australia. The Green Party of the United States helped with the development of the Global Green Charter and initiated the Global Green Coordination resolution.

More importantly, we are constructing an active committee to work on global issues, global action campaigns and global initiatives. In fact, a few months ago, together with Pressure Point and Friends of the Earth in Australia, we led a global Green day of action against EXXON/MOBIL. This Global Green boycott was introduced and endorsed in Australia at the Global Green conference and many other Green Parties around the world participated in this important boycott with the main purpose of addressing global warming.

The Green Party of the United States has maintained its *green* color. The importance of the environment is integrated into our whole Green political agenda. Democracy must be reinstated for us to become effective in our push for a healthier environment.

The current trend of dismantling democracy is done by the hold that multinational companies have over our elections and commonwealth. As the United States government has become more entrenched in its connection to the corporate world, injustices and gross poverty increase.

With the recent good news of our FEC filing on November 8, 2001, we can really start pushing our green agenda even more. We did very well this year in the elections, with 48 newly elected public officials. We still have a long way to go, but we are determined and committed. We understand the importance of our position due to the fact that this is the most powerful country in the world from where many environmental problems stem. The Green Party of the United States is here to stay. It will grow and be ready to move into power, and, with this we take our green roots—our dedication to addressing the needs of the environment—to making this world a greener place.

Corporations and the Environment:
Strong Environmental Laws Remain Critical

Laura Goldin

Even as the rest of the international community moves forward on a landmark protocol to address global warming, the United States is regressing in protecting its environment at home. By whatever name—free trade and capital mobility, national security, economic stimulus—the current Administration effectively is attempting to weaken a successful tool for environmental protection—our federal environmental laws. The Bush administration's proposals essentially translate to loosening requirements on American industry. Going forward with these measures would be a critical misstep, and would undermine a legal system that has proven its potency in protecting the environment.

The enactment of the National Environmental Policy Act (NEPA) in 1970 (signed into law by President Richard M. Nixon) kicked off the adoption over the next 20-odd years of a complex web of environmental laws. These laws were triggered by the dawning realization, eloquently expressed by environmental pioneer Rachel Carson in *Silent Spring*, of the serious environmental pitfalls of post-war industrialization. The enormous shift to large-scale agricultural production fueled by pesticides and fertilizers, the rapidly growing reliance on gas-burning automobiles, the explosion of manufactured goods for mass-market consumption—all of these were visibly taking their toll. As we headed into the late 1960s and 1970s, Los Angeles— once the land of sun and clear skies—was increasingly the land of crowded freeways and frequent blankets of dismal, choking smog. Northeastern forests and lakes were suffering from acid rain caused by midwestern steel mills, utilities and other coal-burning industries. Plumes of toxic wastes leaching from landfills and factories, particularly in the major industrialized areas, were seen in the ominous rainbow colors of rivers and streams, tasted in drinking water and linked with serious human health effects.

The new environmental laws were a strong, if perhaps somewhat naïve and clumsy, assault on reversing this destructive trend. One by one, the problems were targeted by new federal legislation: The Clean Air Act; the Clean Water Act; the Safe Drinking Water Act; the Toxic Substances Control Act (TSCA); the Resource, Conservation and Recovery Act (RCRA); the "Superfund" Law; and so on. The laws were then fleshed out gradually in thousands of pages of EPA regulations, which continue to be promulgated and modified as the agency addresses each problem area. We have recurring opportunities to make legislative adjustments, since each law generally requires reauthorization by Congress every few years. The resulting regulatory scheme targets chemicals from "cradle to grave," spanning manufacture, use, transportation and disposal. It imposes limitations on emissions into air and water, creates employee and public "right to know" about chemicals present in workplaces and neighborhoods, and enables emergency planning for chemical disasters like the Bhopal, India Union Carbide tragedy.

There is no doubt that the federal laws and regulations are imperfect and do not entirely satisfy anyone. In general, environmentalists urge broader and more stringent standards, while industry argues the standards are overly restrictive. All might reasonably agree, however, that at best they are complex; at worst, poorly drafted, overly focused on paperwork requirements rather than substantive controls, and sometimes even arguably based on "bad science." A common complaint is that the laws produce unnecessary, costly and duplicative requirements for record keeping and reporting, and that the government never even looks at the filed paperwork. In part these flaws are due to the nature of the promulgation process—the laws and regulations are the product of significant debate and compromise, and necessarily based only on the limits of our current scientific understanding. Even environmentalists agree that the system could be streamlined to better target actual environmental goals, such as specific reductions in chemical use and quality of air and water emissions.

Despite their many weaknesses, however, these laws have made an enormous difference. As we begin the 21st century, many areas affected by environmental regulations have cleaner air, water, and soils. The Charles River flowing by the Brandeis campus is a prime example—from a repository of raw sewage, wastewater effluent and debris, it has become, in parts, a sometimes fishable and even swimmable haven. The Charles and many other natural resource gems owe their successful recovery primarily to stringent environmental laws and regulations, including Massachusetts' own robust wetlands protection scheme. The laws gave teeth to the requirements by subjecting violators to potentially high civil penalties and even criminal liability. They also gave clout to individual citizens and environmental activist groups, who can act as the regulatory agencies' watchdogs and file claims against violators. Thus, the Charles River owes its renewed health not only to vigorous enforcement by the EPA and its state counterpart, the

DEP, but also to the hard work and commitment
of concerned individuals and effective environmental
organizations like the Charles River Watershed
Association.

The laws did their job particularly well in affecting
industry practices. Companies who routinely dumped
chemical wastes into streams behind their properties
and down drains in their shop floors now had to treat,
collect, or otherwise properly dispose of their wastewater.
Factories spewing noxious fumes now had to install
"scrubbers" or other "best available control technologies"
to reduce air pollutants rather than merely build taller
and taller smokestacks. Companies with old leaking
and rotting underground oil, gasoline, and chemical
storage tanks now had to remove and replace them
with leak-resistant materials and design and clean up
any contamination. "Environmental Manager" became
a whole new professional job category as complex
regulations spelled out new required permits and
licenses; chemical labeling, segregation and containment,
limitations on hazardous waste storage, etc. For the
first time, industry became required by statute to
clean up hazardous waste sites polluted by their own
chemical wastes — sites like Love Canal, New York; and
Silresim, Industriplex and Baird & McGuire right here in
Massachusetts.

The resulting burden on industry was by no means
welcomed. Indeed, it was a slow and painful process as
companies and trade groups representing industry went
"kicking and screaming" into compliance after many
legal challenges and angry meetings with government
officials. In the late 1970s and early 1980s, it was
not uncommon to encounter senior company managers

who just didn't accept that the new requirements applied to their businesses, and were unwilling to put adequate resources — whether money, staff, equipment or management focus — toward compliance. Once companies finally hired environmental managers to address the requirements of the new laws, these employees typically were placed very low on the totem pole — reporting through several layers of plant hierarchy with inadequate budget, clout or training. (Even now the subtle and not-so-subtle industry pressure is on to loosen the current requirements and oppose any new ones, through congressional lobbying, campaign contributions, public relations campaigns and other means.)

What happened to make a difference? The laws proved to have the teeth and claws of stringent requirements and potential for strong civil and criminal enforcement. Many companies found themselves facing enormous fines for environmental violations—fines that could not easily be absorbed as a routine cost of doing business. In more egregious cases, the EPA and the Department of Justice wielded their criminal authority — hauling white-collar CEOs into court like the cheating Wall Street brokers of the 1980s. State attorneys general also used state criminal laws to obtain indictments and convictions. Companies who were caught faced public relations nightmares, affecting relations with customers, investors, and employees. Eventually even industry dinosaurs submitted to the inevitable need to make an effort toward compliance, as public support rallied behind environmental protection and the courts upheld the major laws. (The courts even ruled, for example, that Superfund's imposition of retroactive liability for hazardous waste clean-up costs passed constitutional muster— even though the wastes were disposed of entirely in accordance with all legal requirements at the time of the disposal.) A spate of "toxic tort" cases, like those portrayed in the best selling book, *A Civil Action*, and the movie, *Erin Brockovich*, also highlighted the potential for serious human health effects from industry's failure to handle chemicals properly.

The bottom line—detailed requirements and strict enforcement—worked. Company dollars finally were loosed to hire qualified professionals with sufficient clout to get the job done. They were authorized to put in place environmental management systems and install needed pollution abatement equipment. (Many of the early company environmental managers point to criminal enforcement as the best thing that ever happened to them—senior company managers started paying attention.) As changes were made, many companies even began to see the *benefits* of compliance. Reducing reliance on toxic chemicals was cheaper in the long run, minimizing purchasing, handling and disposal costs and potential future liability. Human Resource managers noted that employees working in clean and secure environments worked more productively and had fewer lost workdays and worker compensation claims. They also found that "doing good" was good for business—that it went hand-in-hand with effective company-wide management, good community and employee relations, and positive public and customer image and investor security.

As we begin the 21st Century, Corporate Environmental Management has matured to a sophisticated field of study and practice, a subject of industry-driven voluntary international standards, and an enormously profitable economic opportunity for consultants, manufacturers of environmental control technologies and many others. Most major industries include environmental commitment as one of their most basic business goals. They tout their environmental commitment, asserting that their environmentalism goes well beyond mere legal compliance to proactive controls and community outreach programs. According to their advertising and public relations pronouncements, one might even imagine that they are in the business of environmental protection.

But let's be realistic. Environmental compliance does not directly contribute to the bottom line. Company VPs responsible for increasing profit margins still view this kind of government regulation as a burdensome, "administrative" cost. Otherwise, why would ex-Vice President Dan Quayle and his "Anti-Competitiveness Council" target environmental regulations as a hindrance to international competition? Why do affected industries lobby so vehemently against each proposed tightening of environmental regulatory controls—reformulated gasoline standards, "cleaner cars" requirements, tightened standards for power plant emissions—just to name a few? Why did industry quickly threaten suit against ex-President Clinton's parting approval of the EPA's new clean air rules for heavy trucks and buses (estimated to reduce smog by 90% over the next decade by limiting tailpipe emissions and forcing refiners to reduce the sulfur in diesel fuel)? When the economy turns downward and money gets tight, environmental compliance is one of the first things to go—ask any in-house environmental manager or attorney.

So streamlining, simplification, elimination of duplication—these are all good goals for legislators and environmental regulators in this and future administrations. But the laws are doing their job well. We have cleaner air, purer water, and reasonably effective systems for controlling use of toxic materials and cleaning up hazardous waste sites. We must support vigorously our hard-won environmental laws to ensure focus on the ultimate goal—a cleaner and more healthful world for all.

III. Greens and Global Environmental Politics

The Kyoto Protocol and Global Environmental Challenges
Grace Akumu

Until the Green Movement and Green Parties pushed
environmental issues nationally and internationally,
other parties and governments used to make only casual
references to environmental problems.

It is now acknowledged that environmental issues must
be taken seriously if the world is to remain a safe place
to live. Thanks mainly to the Greens, the world convened
a global conference in Rio de Janeiro in 1992, where
a number of conventions dealing with environmental
issues were signed. These were: the United Nations
Framework Convention on Climate Change (UNFCCC)—
which later gave birth to the Kyoto Protocol in 1997,
the UN Convention to Combat Desertification (UNCCD),
and the UN Convention on Biodiversity (UNCBD). Apart
from these major achievements, world governments
realized that it is also necessary to include environmental
protection in all multilateral agreements. It is important
to note that the sustainable development goal of the UN
Conference on Environment and Development (UNCED)
process will remain a mirage if issues dealing with equity,
adequacy of commitments by industrialized countries,
such as those on greenhouse emissions reductions, and
financial and technology transfer, are not implemented.
Equally, the principle of common but differentiated
responsibilities must be dealt with head-on.

The priority in the Kyoto Protocol for developing countries is the linking of environment and development. This was the whole purpose of the Rio UNCED Conference. Yet, for industrialized countries, the main issue or priority in the Protocol is greenhouse gas (GHG) emissions reductions. These two different priorities have presented a serious challenge in the climate change negotiations and will continue to do so for some time. Moreover, the successful implementation of the Protocol will be undermined by these two competing priorities, which already divide the Northern and Southern hemispheres in the climate change and Kyoto Protocol negotiations. The main challenge will be how to intertwine the environment and development and not separate them.

Out of UNCED also came Agenda 21 which covered various aspects of protecting the environment, for example the atmosphere, biodiversity, deserts, forests, water, etc. The UNCED conference went much further and discussed a global, and not national, coalition for the conservation of the human environment. A most important principle that came out of Rio is the global resolution to promote sustainable development, with equity being the underlying principle.

Climate change is an equity issue in the Convention (UNFCCC). Article 3.1 states *inter alia*:

"Parties should protect the climate system for the benefit of present and future generations of humankind, on the basis of equity and in accordance with their common but differentiated responsibilities and respective capabilities. Accordingly, developed country Parties should take the lead in combating climate change and the adverse effects thereof."

However, what has been witnessed in the negotiations of the Kyoto Protocol is the erosion of the commitments to reduce GHG emissions. For example, the Second Assessment Report from the Intergovernmental Panel on Climate Change (IPCC) talks about reduction of GHG emissions by at least 60 percent by 2050. Yet, in the Kyoto Protocol agreement of 1997, industrialized countries agreed to reduce their GHG emissions by only five percent below their 1990 levels in the commitment period 2008-12. Even this five percent may be grossly undermined by the superfluous sink credits given for carbon sequestration, which countries can apply instead of reduction of emissions. Even top global scientists agree to their scientific uncertainty in carbon sequestration to date.

The above figures clearly raise the issue of adequacy of commitments both in the Convention and the Protocol. However, despite recent attempts it has not been possible to bring this to the agenda. This also raises the issue of adaptation to the adverse effects of climate change as developing countries have no adaptive capacity and are most vulnerable. As stated in the Third Assessment Report of the IPCC, Africa will suffer the most from the impacts of climate change. Yet this is a region the average per capita income of which is less than $300 per year. Therefore, without serious commitments to *development* first and foremost, while addressing emissions reductions, regions such as Africa will soon be overwhelmed by adverse impacts due to their vulnerability. Experiences of the devastation of Cuba by Hurricane Mitchel in 2001, the destruction in Central America, where countries like Nicaragua and Honduras suffered severe damages in 1997 with deaths, loss of property, and harm to infrastructure, and the severe damages in Mozambique, are all still fresh in our minds. Asia has also recently had its share of damages especially in Bangladesh, China, and India.

Developing countries presently face a host of challenges in adapting to climate change. A number of them have recently been experiencing adverse impacts ranging from extreme weather events to flooding and drought, both with their attendant consequences. Some of the consequences have been increase in weather-related diseases such as malaria, typhoid, cholera, as well as food insecurity, infrastructure damages, and electricity shortages. Yet the UNFCCC states in Art.2 that the ultimate objective of the Convention and any other related instruments is to achieve stabilization of GHG emissions in the atmosphere at a level that would prevent dangerous anthropogenic interference with the climate system. Such levels should be achieved within a time frame sufficient to allow ecosystems to adapt naturally to climate change, to ensure that food production is not threatened and to enable economic development to proceed in a sustainable manner.

Many developing countries are currently experiencing negative growth rates as well as deficits in food production. African countries are some of the hardest hit.

Also, during the 2001 negotiations on the implementation of the Kyoto Protocol (UNFCCC-COP 6) in Bonn, Germany, only a few industrialized countries, such as the governments of Switzerland, Canada, Norway, Iceland, as well as the European Union, agreed to contribute the equivalent of US$410 million over a period of five years to the Climate Change Funds.

Such lack of commitment and political will on the part of industrialized countries for the effective implementation of adaptation measures under the Kyoto Protocol challenge the success of all agreements. Meanwhile, a UNEP/industry group has stated that it would cost approximately US$300 billion per year to compensate for climate change-related damages in the Northern hemisphere. Comparing this to the paltry US$410 million which was proposed at COP6 for adaptation and other climate programs in the developing countries, one notes the very serious lack of commitment on the part of the industrialized countries. Moreover, diversion of the already declining *Official Development Assistance* (ODA) to implement both the Convention and Kyoto Protocol would expose the serious lack of political will on the part of the North to combat climate change.

The other major challenge is that whereas industrialized countries have the capacity to adapt to the impacts, developing countries do not. Also, developed countries have compensation in the form of insurance benefits for the damages caused to them by these adverse impacts whereas in the developing countries, such compensation is non-existent.

One of the greatest challenges, however, has been the recent U.S. withdrawal from the Kyoto Protocol with the statement that it is fatally flawed and will damage its economy, and that developing countries must also take up commitments to reduce their GHG emissions. The U.S. Government has tried repeatedly to raise this issue in the negotiations despite the fact that the Convention states clearly that developing country emissions "are still relatively low and that the share of global emissions originating in developing countries will still have to grow in order to meet their social and development needs." Moreover, a number of studies conducted already by various groups both within and outside the U.S., reveal that developing countries are actually doing a lot to reduce their emissions. The energy sector in China is an example. The Chinese are moving towards efficiency despite the fact they still have no reduction commitments in the Convention.

Our planet and its people are set to experience further dire consequences if global temperatures continue to rise with no significant action taken on GHG emissions reductions. The ever increasingly unsustainable and inequitable development path the world is pursuing needs to be urgently addressed. Twenty percent of the world's population living in the industrialized countries cannot continue to indiscriminately pollute the atmosphere at the expense of the majority. Regions such as Africa only consume two to three percent of the global energy total and therefore have negligible GHG emissions to reduce. It is said that Africa only emits subsistence GHG emissions. A sampling of what happens in some industrialized countries attests to this. Sample this: "New York uses more gasoline in a week than the whole of Africa does in a year. There are more cars in Westphalia, Germany, than in the whole of Africa. Texas alone, with a population of 30 million, emits more CO2 than 93 developing countries added together, with a combined population of nearly one billion people, and nearly three times as much CO2 as Brazil. Even Maine, the U.S. lowest emitting state, with a two million population, emits more CO2 than 41 developing countries combined, whose total population comes to 110 million" (*ECO Publication*, November 1998). The challenge is to consume sustainably and to get away from "the U.S. lifestyle is non-negotiable syndrome" which the 41st President of the United States, George Bush Senior, stated in Rio de Janeiro in 1992 during the Earth Summit.

The use of sinks in the flexibility mechanisms (because of their being *low-hanging fruits* or a cheaper option for industrialized countries to reducing their GHG emissions) is a sure way to undermine the environmental integrity of and effective implementation of the Kyoto Protocol. Emissions trading and the weak compliance system are bound to make the Protocol hot air.

The Kyoto Protocol is market-based. Yet it is now clear from experience in developing countries that the market alone cannot bring solutions to all the environment and development challenges. A deliberate mix of approaches must be examined and applied. The market alone is already extensively marginalizing regions such as Africa, where, for over 40 years, development has eluded the continent. Therefore, the Kyoto Protocol must strive to address inequity in order to succeed. It should not be forgotten that in 1997, the year the Kyoto Protocol came into existence, foreign direct investment zoomed to US$400 billion, seven times the level of the 1970s, but 58% of it went to industrial countries, 37% to developing countries, and 5% to Transition Economies of Eastern Europe and the Commonwealth of Independent States (CIS), with the top fifth of the world's people in the richest countries enjoying 82% of the expanding export trade and 68% of foreign direct investment—the bottom fifth, barely more than 1%. These trends reinforce economic stagnation and low human development (*UNDP Human Development Report*, 1999).

Africa is fully convinced that environment and development should be tackled in an integrated manner. In this regard, industrialized countries must begin to pay fair prices for commodities from developing countries and the current humiliating trade imbalances must be rectified. Otherwise, poverty reduction will forever remain a mirage. In the Climate Change Convention, developing countries have stated that economic and social development and poverty eradication are their first and overriding priorities. The main challenge therefore being how to meet the objectives of the Convention and alleviate poverty.

In their latest effort to accelerate Africa's development, African leaders have adopted the *New African Initiative*. In the declaration, Art.54.8, termed 'The Environment Initiative,' they have emphasized combating desertification, wetland conservation, invasive alien species, coastal management and global warming.

One of the most important multilateral agreements for Africa are the African-Caribbean-Pacific and European Union partnership agreement, the last of which was signed in Cotonou, Bennin, West Africa on 23 June 2000. Art.32 states:

1. Cooperation on environmental protection and sustainable utilization and management of natural resources shall aim at:

a) Mainstreaming environmental sustainability into all aspects of development cooperation and support programs and projects implemented by various actors

b) Building and/or strengthening the scientific, technical, human and institutional capacity for environmental management for all environmental stakeholders

c) Supporting specific measures and schemes aimed at addressing critical sustainable management issues and also relating to current and future regional and international commitments concerning minerals and natural resources such as:

i) tropical forest, water resources, coastal, marine and fisheries resources, wildlife, soils, biodiversity

ii) protection of fragile ecosystems, e.g. coral reefs

iii) renewable energy sources, notably solar, and energy efficiency

iv) sustainable rural and urban development

v) desertification, drought and deforestation

vi) developing innovative solutions to urban environmental problems and

vii) promotion of sustainable tourism

d) Taking into account issues relating to the transport and disposal of hazardous wastes

2. Cooperation shall also take account of:

a) The vulnerability of small island ACP countries, especially to the threat posed by climate change

b) The worsening drought and desertification problems especially of least developed countries and land-locked countries, and

c) Institutional development and capacity building.

I have quoted Art. 32 extensively and in full because of the importance Africa attaches to it. Yet African environmentalists are of the opinion that most of Africa's environmental problems were, and are still, being worsened by industrialized countries, especially their transnational companies which are mining, drilling and logging in Africa. As a result, environmental deterioration in Africa has moved from bad to worse. Moreover, due to internationally skewed trade in favor of industrialized countries, regions such as Africa will never be able to overcome developmental and environmental obstacles.

Equally, despite Art. 32 above being very well crafted, just as other articles in other global agreements, African environmentalists are of the opinion that without an effective globally agreed compliance system, these agreements will only remain in bookshelves for research purposes and not for implementation and realization on the ground.

Today the world is awash with international environmental agreements, but none with an effective compliance system.

Most developing countries lack the capacity to participate and implement global environmental agreements; consequently critical decisions are taken without their full knowledge and effective participation. In order to minimize global environmental challenges and threats, effective long-term processes that would require the strengthening of both human and institutional capacities are urgently required in the Southern hemisphere.

Some of the global environmental threats, climate change for example, are a challenge for both industrialized and developing countries, and all stakeholders alike. Since cooperation to combat it is required from all, lack of awareness is an obstacle to getting fully involved in the process.

The mobilization of the populations at all levels is therefore necessary in order to develop appropriate responses. Article 6 of the Climate Change Convention, which deals with public awareness and education, therefore needs to be urgently implemented.

It is important that the Green Movement, together with like-minded people, form an international organization to coordinate green campaigns for a better world by starting an intensive global campaign, creating a functioning network, regular meetings, and regional chapters—especially in Africa where poverty has driven environmental issues to the bottom of the agenda.

The Two Sides of Globalization: Global Citizen's Movements Face Down Multinational Corporations to Protect Wilderness

Ari Hershowitz

I am the director of the BioGems Initiative in Latin America, a project of the Natural Resources Defense Council, or NRDC. NRDC has thirty years of experience in science and law based advocacy on behalf of the environment. We combine this experience and technical ability with the strength of more than half a million members in the United States and Canada. The BioGems Initiative identifies important natural areas in the Americas that are under threat, where our members and the coordinated action of people around the world can make a difference. A number of these campaigns highlight the struggle between major multinational corporations and democracy over the resources of this planet. These are the central opposing forces of globalization, and I will discuss two prime examples of this struggle.

The BioGems Initiative was born out of the major international campaign to save San Ignacio Lagoon in Baja California, Mexico. San Ignacio Lagoon is the world's last undisturbed gray whale nursery: Gray whales take a 5,000 mile journey to this lagoon in the winter to mate, to give birth, and to train their young. It is a magical place, where gray whales approach humans to make contact, and it is one of the best preserved coastal desert lagoon ecosystems in the world. It is one of the most protected areas on the planet: It includes a national park, whale sanctuary, bird sanctuary, part of Latin America's largest

Biosphere Reserve, and a United Nations designated World Heritage Site, to be protected as a natural treasure for future generations.

It is also where Mitsubishi Corporation, one of the biggest companies on earth wanted to build the world's largest industrial salt factory. Mitsubishi wanted the salt—20,000 tons a day, eight million tons a year—to feed its chemical factories in Japan, as raw material from which to make chlorine. The factory would flood 116 square miles surrounding the lagoon—twice the area of Washington, D.C.—with increasingly concentrated saltwater tanks, and dump twenty million tons of toxic brine into the lagoon each day. The project would include a one and a half mile long pier into the ocean, in the direct path of migrating gray whale mothers and calves, to dock enormous ocean-going supertankers, which would carry the salt away. Mitsubishi's local subsidiary, in partnership with the Mexican government, would harvest the salt and sell it for $15 a ton to the parent corporation which would make it into chlorine worth $200 per ton.

Mitsubishi's political influence was very strong, with Mexico's powerful minister of trade and numerous local politicians determined to make sure that the salt works was built. The small, proud communities of San Ignacio Lagoon, which make their living from fishing and nature-based tourism, opposed the project as a threat to their fisheries and way of life. A few national figures, including activist and poet Homero Aridjis, president of the environmental organization Grupo de los Cien, began to stir national opposition to the project.

The Mexican Green Party became involved early on, making contacts with local communities, and beginning to look into environmental practices at an existing salt works plant Mitsubishi operates about 100 miles north of San Ignacio Lagoon. This soon became the basis for an extensive Mexican Congressional hearing that was instrumental in highlighting the poor economics of this project, and creating opposition from local communities.

The Natural Resources Defense Council was asked by these communities and several groups in Mexico to bring this threat to international attention. It helped to develop an extensive network of organizations and individuals around the world concerned with protecting this special place.

As a result, NRDC, along with the International Fund for Animal Welfare joined together with groups in Mexico to form the international *Coalition to Save Laguna San Ignacio (Coalicion Para la Defensa de Laguna San Ignacio)*. More than 50 Mexican groups, including Grupo de los Cien, UGAM (the Union of Environmental Groups of Mexico), CEMDA (Mexican Environmental Law Center), and ProEsteros were part of this growing Coalition, whose legal and political efforts in Mexico were coordinated by Alberto Szekely, one of Mexico's leading environmental lawyers, and Andrés Rozental, who had served as Mexican Ambassador to Great Britain and also as the Mexican government representative to the International Whaling Commission.

The groups which made up the *Coalition to Save Laguna San Ignacio* were located throughout Mexico and the United States. Later in the campaign, European and, to some degree, Japanese activists also became engaged. The ultimate success of the campaign was built, in part, on this geographic coverage. ProEsteros, a Baja California-based wetlands conservation group, was able to both represent the concerns of local environmentalists on a world stage and provide information to the Coalition about local reaction in Baja California to the growing international controversy. Similarly, IFAW, with its offices worldwide, and NRDC, with its large membership in the United States, were able to mobilize tremendous international support for Mexican groups and also leverage this support to influence decision-making in Mexico.

Through direct mail outreach, widely publicized yearly missions to the lagoon, appeals to the World Heritage Committee, and numerous other activities, the Coalition kept the debate in regular public view. The pressure on Mitsubishi and the Mexican government to abandon plans for the salt works built steadily within Mexico and abroad to the point that in November of 1999, *Newsweek* reported that the situation was "looking more like Mitsubishi against the world."

The Coalition Campaign
The Coalition's multipronged strategy included:

• Legal challenges in Mexico

• A broad media campaign in Mexico, with newspaper advertising, billboards, radio interviews, and a large music concert held in Mexico City.

• A massive public education effort: millions of pieces of mail were sent as a part of this effort

- International scientific consensus: a statement by 34 world-renowned scientists, including nine Nobel Prize winners, called the salt works an "unacceptable risk" to the ecosystems of San Ignacio Lagoon

- Hard-hitting advertisements in the United States, Mexico, Europe and Japan

- Yearly missions to San Ignacio Lagoon with Mexican political figures, celebrities, opinion leaders, Coalition members, and the media

- Appeals to the United Nations World Heritage Committee to designate San Ignacio Lagoon a "World Heritage Site in Danger"

- A Mitsubishi "Don't Buy It" consumer action campaign, targeting all Mitsubishi products

- Pressure within the European Parliament to link the Mitsubishi salt works to negotiations on the Europe-Mexico Free Trade Agreement

- A web-based campaign, with websites in English (www.nrdc.org, www.savebajawhales.com) and Spanish (www.coalicionsanignacio.org)

Mitsubishi received mountain loads of mail opposing their salt works plans, including hundreds of drawings and cards from schoolchildren across the country. One familiar refrain among these children's cards was "How would you feel if someone built a huge salt works in your home?" The stream of mail increased as the campaign continued, and Mitsubishi took note. By the end of the campaign, we estimate that Mitsubishi received more than a million letters, in addition to thousands of emails and faxes from around the world, calling for the cancellation of the salt works.

In Mexico, in the summer of 1998, the Coalition unrolled a sophisticated public outreach strategy with Coalition members appearing on television and radio talk shows almost weekly to explain the Coalition's views on the salt works and to update an interested public on the continuing saga of the campaign. News reports and features in Mexico on the campaign became more and more frequent, with an average of approximately three daily reports in the national media on the campaign.

In March of 1999, after a five-year campaign that stretched from a small rural Mexican fishing village around the world, Mexico's President Ernesto Zedillo announced the cancellation of plans for the salt works. Mitsubishi followed suit the same day. The last undisturbed gray whale lagoon on earth, and the global citizens network that developed to protect it, had won.

This was not only a major victory for nature, but also for democracy. It was one of the first steps in the full democratization of Mexico, a process that continued shortly afterward with the election that forced the ruling political party, the PRI, out of the Presidential seat for the first time in the history of modern Mexico.

It was also a victory over the destructive forces of globalization. Today, the ability to stop these forces is being tested again, in the small Central American country of Belize.

Fortis, Inc., an energy and real estate company based in St. John's, Newfoundland, plans to build a 150-foot high concrete hydroelectric dam on the Macal River in Belize. The "Chalillo" dam would flood the Macal River Valley, one of the last intact wilderness areas in Central America, and habitat for more than a dozen rare and endangered species, including the jaguar, the tapir—Belize's national animal—and a subspecies of Scarlet Macaw that is only found in Northern Central America. Scientists estimate that fewer than 200 of this rare subspecies of bird are left in Belize, and 1000 in the entire region. Fortis' wildlife consultant for this project, the Natural History Museum of London, found that the dam would cause the probable "extirpation" of this bird from Belize.

Eighteen of the world's leading forest experts and ecologists, including Dr. David Suzuki and Dr. Peter Raven, President of the American Association for the Advancement of Science, wrote to Mr. Marshall, CEP of Fortis, Inc., stating that the dam would cause "significant and long lasting" impacts on ecosystems and species of the region, and calling plans for the dam "reckless." The Natural History Museum reported, among other effects, that the dam would cause "significant and irreversible reduction in biological diversity in Belize...fragmentation of the proposed Mesoamerican Biological Corridor" and a reduction in the numbers of migratory birds from the United States and Canada.

The dam is not only an environmental travesty, but also an economic disaster for the people of Belize. Fortis, Inc. controls both energy production and energy distribution in Belize, charging Belizeans more than three times the electricity rates of consumers in Canada. These high costs are largely due to the "Mollejon" dam, a smaller facility Fortis owns downstream from the proposed dam. Fortis' profit margin is more than four times higher for electricity sold in Belize. The contract for the new dam would force the people of Belize to pay more than half a billion dollars over 50 years to Fortis for a meager amount of electricity.

The Belize Alliance of Conservation NGO's, a coalition of environmental groups in Belize, asked NRDC to help them stop this destructive project in late 1999. This campaign, in many ways presents a more fundamental challenge to our ability to protect nature from corporate globalization. The multinational corporation in this case, Fortis Inc. of Newfoundland, has a limited presence globally, with few operations outside of Atlantic Canada.

This campaign, too, has involved international treaties: at the World Conservation Congress in Amman, Jordan, the International Union for the Conservation of Nature (IUCN) unanimously approved a resolution on the Protection of the Macal River Valley, describing the threats posed by the dam. Environmental groups from Belize, the United States, Canada, and England have gotten involved. A sign-on letter from a dozen of these groups to Stan Marshall urged the cancellation of the project. There has also been increasing media and international attention: The issue has been covered in the *New York Times*, the major national newspapers and television news programs in Canada, as well as local coverage in Newfoundland and Belize. Demonstrations in Newfoundland at Fortis' Annual Shareholder meeting, and in Belize's capital city of Belmopan, gathering more than 400 protesters, has maintained the spotlight on this important issue. Actor Harrison Ford, who filmed *The Mosquito Coast* in Belize has spoken out against the project, and wrote a widely read editorial in the *Toronto Globe and Mail*. A coalition website www.stopfortis.org provides a full record of the campaign, and hosts a growing petition of hundreds of signatures from around the world.

The Green Party in Mexico raised this issue in the Mexican parliament and has pursued this threat to regional biodiversity in public discussions in major Mexican newspapers. As a result of discussions stemming from the Conference on International Greens at Brandeis in November 2001, Arnold Cassola, President of the EU Green Parties, worked with parliamentarians to present questions in the EU Parliament about the project, and the impacts of this project on the Convention on Biodiversity and EU-funded activities in Belize.

As international public awareness grows, so, it seems, does the determination of Fortis and the government of Belize to go ahead with the dam project. The company's stated goal was to begin construction in January 2002.

In fact, the company did begin construction illegally on January 15, without permits and without any public hearings. The Belize Alliance of Conservation NGOs has now brought a lawsuit in Belize challenging the government's "conditional approval" for the project. On February 28, 2002, BACONGO won the first round: the Chief Justice granted leave to hear the case. The arguments should begin in the next few weeks.

This issue is a true test of the ability of global citizen's movements to protect important wilderness areas from the most insidious consequences of globalization. The Laguna San Ignacio Campaign shows that global victories for the environment are possible.

This is an urgent matter, and I ask help from all of you to protect this special place.

Visit www.stopfortis.org to learn more, and sign the petition to protect the Macal River Valley.

"Beyond this conflict (…) the further destiny of the United States is being shaped by mass poverty, mass illiteracy, mass disease and massive environmental disruption. The people of the United States realize this. They know that we cannot protect our future by turning our backs on it. In that knowledge they are well ahead of at least part of the political system."

Professor Leon Furth, former National Security Advisor to Al Gore

The Double Nexus of Security, Globalization and Sustainable Development
Sascha Müller-Kraenner

September 11 has made it clear that there will no longer be two zones of different security in the world. The democratic, rich and safe countries of the North cannot insulate themselves from lawnessness, poverty and insecure countries in other world regions. The current effort of the United States and its allies to fight terrorism, its supporters and its support structures in a multilateral coalition and with a mix of military, economic, diplomatic, and humanitarian instruments should lead to a new global security architecture and replace, step by step, regional arrangements that have separated the world into safe and unsafe places. The complexity of this strategy and the character of the multilateral approach as such implies that any new security framework will not rely on military and geopolitical components alone but has to include a broad range of reforms in governance and international cooperation.

This raises the question whether the new global security architecture will replace current globalization tendencies or be integrated with them. The economic globalization of the last decade has been criticized for doing damage to the environment and the poor. Institutions that play a prominent role in globalization, like the World Bank, the International Monetary Fund, and the World Trade Organization were accused of lacking democratic accountability. It is an open question whether the new emphasis on regional stability and security will enforce current globalization trends or lead to a stronger focus on human development, social cohesion, and good governance in developing countries.

The World Summit on Sustainable Development in Johannesburg will take place exactly one year after the terrorist attacks of September 11. The summit provides a unique opportunity to discuss globalization from a sustainable development perspective. Whether this perspective is still being asked for depends on whether we can make a convincing argument that sustainable development contributes to a positive economic perspective in all regions and to the political stability of the international system.

To make the double nexus between a new international security architecture, globalization and sustainable development is partly an intellectual exercise. A vague awareness exists that unsustainable development patterns are intensified by globalization patterns and thereby increasingly contribute to regional instabilities. The task of the environment and development movements will be, however, to develop concrete proposals and instruments for redefining this double connection.

For quite a while, environmental policy has not been a top concern for global policy makers. The Kyoto agreement on climate change proved to be an exception. The final success of the Kyoto negotiations at the Bonn climate summit also showed that complex environmental negotiations can only be resolved if heads of government pay adequate attention to those processes and if they are perceived in a broader political context.

When heads of government have to make the decision whether to participate in the Johannesburg summit and whether to invest the necessary political capital to make it a success, they will make this decision based on the following questions:

• Is there a clear agenda?

• Will there be achievable results?

• Are the results relevant to my core constituencies?

At this point, the answer to all three questions is "no." Must the agenda of Johannesburg therefore be changed? The answer is obviously yes—but most of all a new urgency should be injected into the negotiations. The preparations for Johannesburg in the Commission on Sustainable Development had a slow start. Now, in a new context, time has become an even more critical factor. Johannesburg has to advertise itself as "the" forum where globalization—on an unprecedented scale—will be discussed between the world's governments and civil society.

After September 11, the question was raised whether the Johannesburg summit should go ahead as planned. It was argued that the security situation and the shift in international priorities should lead to a postponement or even a cancellation of the summit. However, as the climate conference in Marrakesh (Morocco) and the World Trade Summit in Doha (Qatar) have shown, the security concerns can be addressed. Some have even argued that the current climate of cooperation in the aftermath of September 11 can lead to swift political agreements to overcome technical difficulties in a lot of international arenas. Even before September 11, it was obvious that the World Summit would have to address the nexus between globalization and sustainable development to achieve political relevance. Now the criterion for success must be, that sustainable development makes a significant contribution to a globalization model that increases security both for the North and the South.

The Johannesburg Summit could achieve the following[1]:

Address poverty
It has been widely recognized that, while being not the immediate cause of terrorist acts, the widespread poverty in a number of world regions has provided a fertile breeding ground for radical political ideologies and movements. On the other hand, poverty has contributed to the depletion of resources and has prevented the implementation of environmental legislation in those countries. September 11 has brought home the message that poverty matters not only for humanitarian but also for security reasons.

Example: One of the poverty-related questions that Johannesburg should address is the reduction of hunger. The 1996 World Food Summit has set a target to reduce the number of people who suffer from hunger by 50 percent by the year 2015. Sustainable land use, access to clean energy and water as well as an equitable distribution of those resources can make a significant contribution towards this goal.

Improve governance structures

Dysfunctional states, democratic deficits and an underdeveloped civil society in a number of countries are part of the reason that the sustainable development objectives of Rio could not be achieved. On the other hand, fragmentary and fragile governance structures also result in a lack of security especially for those parts of the population that cannot afford private security services. Environmental governance on the national and international level is only part of a stable system of overall governance and cannot be achieved in isolation. However, environmental governance can make a valuable contribution to the democratic development of communities and the international realm.

Assert the value of international law

The current U.S. administration's rejection of a number of international treaties is an expression of a political analysis that challenges the legitimacy and effectiveness of international law in principle. The rejection of the Kyoto Protocol on Climate Change was just the most spectacular and controversial illustration of this thinking, that is privately being shared by governments and others in a number of countries. The experience of vulnerability after September 11 may lead to a reassessment of the effectiveness of international law as a whole. The willingness of the United States to coordinate the fight against terrorism with an international coalition might make it easier for those in the U.S. elite that have argued continuously that the United States has to accept the legitimacy of international law.

The Kyoto protocol with its high symbolic value is a chance to prove this point. Whether U.S. ratification will be achieved by Johannesburg, when the Protocol is scheduled to enter into force, is doubtful. However, the parties to the Protocol should keep the door open for the United States to join later.

Develop mechanisms to manage the global public goods
In that context the debate on the linkages between environment and security could make a useful contribution.

Strengthen democratic decision making and debating structure
Provide additional financial means to reduce poverty with sustainable development projects and to build functioning governance structures in Southern countries.

How will the debate on globalization change?
Movements critical to globalization had picked up momentum after a series of campaigns around the WTO ministerial conference in Seattle, the EU Summit in Göteburg and the G7 Summit in Genova. The movement had always criticized current U.S. economic policy as contributing significantly to some of the negative

aspects of globalization. The United States has also been accused of throwing its weight around in international institutions and blocking progress in others.

But movements critical to globalization have not only criticized current U.S. policies but also willingly and unwillingly nourished an anti-American ideology. The fashionable anti-Americanism of certain parts of the anti-globalization left is mirrored by parallel developments on the extreme right. Both accuse U.S. Americans of worshipping a materialistic life that stands in stark contrast to the post-materialistic values of the globalization critics and to old traditional cultures both in Europe and in Third World countries.

After September 11, this pattern of argument presents itself in a different context. Naomi Klein, author of *No Logo*, an acclaimed overview of the anti-globalization movement, writes in *The Nation* (October 22, 2001) that "tactics that rely on attacking—even peacefully—powerful symbols of capitalism find themselves in an utterly transformed semiotic landscape." Other activists might put it less eloquently, but the cancellation of planned protests even before the annual World Bank/IMF meeting was cancelled has shown that the anti-globalization movement is deeply unnerved. At a moment when everybody states their public solidarity with the American people, it is almost impossible to paint America as a symbol for everything that is unjust in the world economic order.

Both the (to a relevant part U.S.-led and sponsored) international NGO movement and the UN system will suffer if globalization-critical movements continue to crystallize around an anti-American ideology. Rejecting the ideology of Anti-Americanism is a precondition for globalization-critical movements to enter into a renewed democratic debate with the U.S. government on how the reduction of poverty and the erection of global governance structures can contribute to global economic development and global security.

Will the United States return to multilateralism?

It is frequently stated that, in the aftermath of September 11, the United States and others will rejoin the system of international cooperation. Such a rebirth of multilateralism could provide fertile ground for a "global deal" between environmental interests of the so called "North" and development interests of the "South." However, the current cooperation of the U.S. government with the UN Security Council and the ad hoc coalition with approximately 35 countries to combat terrorism will not automatically inspire a stronger U.S. engagement in other multilateral processes.

There has been a debate over whether September 11 will motivate the U.S. administration to rethink its recent unilateral policies and to return to the multilateral approach of the Clinton administration. In fact, after the terrorist attacks, the United States paid their UN dues, turned to the Security Council for a mandate and asked its allies to invoke Article 5 of the NATO treaty. However, doubts have been raised whether the U.S. effort to build an international coalition against terrorism is more like a multilateralism "a la carte." Some say, that the United States has and will always prefer the flexibility of issue oriented bilateral arrangements to multilateral treaties and institutions.

It is definitely true that average Americans have rediscovered the rest of the world. Whether this increased interest in other countries in the complexities of international relations will translate either into a higher willingness to help developing countries and get involved in international institutions or into a tendency to isolate the United States against newly perceived threats (for example through higher defense spending) has to be shown. Internationalists in the United States and other countries have a window of opportunity to prove to the United States that international cooperation is indispensable and can have a positive impact on U.S. national interests.

[1]http://www.boell.org/docs/WSPaperengl.pdf

List of Contributors

Grace Akumu is the executive director of Climate Network Africa (CNA) based in Nairobi, Kenya, since 1992. CNA is a member of the Climate Action Network (CAN) consortium of NGOs and institutions working on climate change and sustainable development issues. Akumu was graduated from Webster University, Switzerland, in 1987. She majored in international relations. She earned a diploma in French from the University of Fribourg, Switzerland, in 1984. Akumu was one of the lead authors of the Intergovernmental Panel on Climate Change's *Third Assessment Report on Mitigation*. She has also been a technical advisor to Prototype Carbon Fund, World Bank, from 1999 to 2001.

Theresa Amato was graduated from Harvard University in 1986 with a degree in government and economics, and from the New York University School of Law in 1989. Amato was the national campaign manager for the Nader 2000 presidential campaign on the Green Party ticket and is the founder and former executive director (1993-2000) of the Citizen Advocacy Center in Illinois. She is the president of Citizen Works, the newest generation of Ralph Nader-founded organizations.

Arnold Cassola is secretary general of the European Federation of Green Parties. He was elected to this post in 1999. He is also one of the three representatives of the European continent on the Global Green Coordination. He is a cofounder of the Green Party of Malta, "Alternattiva Demokratika" (1989). Cassola is an academic by profession. He has taught at the Universities of Catania (1981-83), Roma "La Sapienza" (1983-88) and Malta (1988-1999) and is the author or editor of numerous publications, including 16 books.

Franz Floss is the international secretary of the Green Party in Austria. He is also the Austrian delegate to the European Greens and a member of the Executive Committee of the Austrian Green Party. An engineer by training, he was previously in charge of consumer information and social issues. He is a food and BSE expert and was the speaker of the European Federation of Green Parties until 2000.

Annie Goeke is the cochair of the International Committee and former cochair of the Steering Committee of the Green Party of the United States. A national delegate from the Green Party of Pennsylvania, Goeke has been involved in Green politics since 1989. She is also an ecofeminist, international peace activist, and an artist. In 2000 she coauthored *Fire Up Your Brilliance*. She recently cofounded the international peace foundation called the Earth Rights Institute—Action Program for a Global Green Agenda.

Laura Goldin is an adjunct assistant professor of environmental studies, associate director of the Environmental Studies Program, and director of the Environmental Internship Program at Brandeis University. She was graduated from Yale University in 1973, and received her J.D. from Cornell Law School and Harvard Law School in 1979. She served as general counsel for the Massachusetts Department of Environmental Protection, where she was the chief environmental lawyer for the state. Before that she was senior environmental attorney for Digital Equipment Corporation's worldwide operations.

Sarah Halpern-Meekin was graduated in May 2002 from Brandeis University with a B.A. in politics. She wrote her senior honors thesis on the consequences of the 1996 welfare reform act.

Ari Hershowitz is the director of the BioGems Project, Latin America, at the Natural Resources Defense Council (NRDC). A scientist by training, Hershowitz was at the forefront of international efforts to protect natural areas, including the global campaign to protect the last undisturbed gray whale nursery in the world—Laguna San Ignacio, in Baja California, Mexico.

Carl Lankowski is director of European Area Studies at the Foreign Service Institute, which is the federal government's primary training institution preparing American diplomats. He previously directed the research program of the American Institute for Contemporary German Studies (AICGS) in Washington, D.C., a policy analysis organization and forum for discussion specializing in comparative public policy, Germany's role in Europe, and transatlantic relations. Prior to that he was a professor of political science at Johns Hopkins University. He has published widely on German and European politics and the effects of globalization.

Sascha Müller-Kraenner has been the director of the Heinrich Böll Foundation in Washington, D.C., since July of 1998. Before that he directed a German League for Nature Conservation and was the chief of staff for a member of the State Legislature in Saxony. He is a graduate in biology and public law from the University in Munich. He previously was a member of the Steering Committee for Climate Network Europe, and was the spokesperson of the Green Party in Bayreuth.

Ralph Nader was graduated from Princeton in 1955, and from Harvard Law School in 1958. A consumer-advocate, he authored many books, including the bestseller *Unsafe at Any Speed* (1965) exposing unsafe cars. Nader was the Green Party nominee for U.S. president in 2000. He received nearly three percent of the popular vote

George Ross is the Morris Hillquit Professor of Labor and Social Thought and director of the Center for German and European Studies at Brandeis University. He is also a senior associate with the Minda de Gunzburg Center for European Studies, Harvard University. He received his Ph.D. in government from Harvard University and has published widely on France and European Integration. He is an editor of *French Politics and Society*, former chair of the West European Politics and Society Section of the American Political Science Association, executive secretary of the Conference Group on French Politics and Society and a member of the European Union's Team Europe in the United States. He served as chair of the Council for European Studies from 1990 to 1997.

Sabine von Mering is assistant professor of German and assistant director for the Center for German and European Studies at Brandeis University. She received her Ph.D. in German studies from the University of California, Davis, in 1998.

Contact Information

The Center for German and European Studies at Brandeis University

The Center for German and European Studies at Brandeis University (CGES-BR) was founded in 1998 by a generous gift from the German government to Brandeis University, the only Jewish-sponsored, nonsectarian, liberal arts, research university in North America. CGES-BR's mission is teaching, research, and outreach to broader communities about the social, political, and cultural issues involved in integrating diversity and difference in Germany and Europe in the new millennium. CGES-BR seeks to promote productive dialogues including many voices about diversity and pluralism in German and European societies, polities and cultures.

Center of German and European Studies
Brandeis University
Olin Sang 205
Mailstop 058
415 South Street
Waltham, MA 02453-2728
781-736-2756
781-736-3207 fax
european@brandeis.edu

The Heinrich Böll Foundation
Headquartered in Berlin, Germany, the Heinrich Böll
Foundation is a political, nonprofit foundation affiliated
with the party of Alliance 90/The Greens. In cooperation
with numerous partner organizations around the world, the
Foundation in its international political education work
aims to strengthen ecology oriented action and civil society
through exchanges. The Foundation's 15 regional offices
worldwide function as hubs of these exchanges, maintaining
close ties with their partner institutions, thus connecting
debates being conducted in Germany and abroad.

Heinrich Böll Foundation
Washington Office
1638 R Street, NW
Suite 120
Washington, DC 20009, USA
202-462-7512
202-262-5230 fax
office@boell.org

The Sustainable International Development Program at Brandeis University
The Sustainable International Development Program of The Heller School for Social Policy and Management at Brandeis University has gained international recognition over the past eight years for its innovation in examining models of development for their achievements in reducing poverty and inequality, in raising quality of life, in enhancing the status of women, and in conserving the biodiversity of fragile environments. Heller seeks fresh thinking about complex relationships, bridging areas of concern reserved traditionally to scientists or social scientists, policy makers, human rights advocates, or development practitioners.

Sustainable International Development Program
Brandeis University
Mailstop 078
P.O. Box 549110
Waltham, MA 02454-9110
781-736-2770
781-736-2774 fax

The Environmental Studies Program at Brandeis University
The Brandeis Environmental Studies Program is an interdisciplinary minor that combines the academic excellence and rigor of Brandeis coursework, faculty, and teaching across the disciplines of the natural and social sciences with a novel, carefully designed hands-on component. Students not only gain broad academic training, but tackle as well actual, complex environmental issues on the Brandeis campus itself and in outside internships alongside highly skilled professionals in industry, public interest, and government. Consistent with the University's underlying commitment to social welfare, the Environmental Studies Program also includes a strong Environmental Justice component.

Environmental Studies Program
Brandeis University
Mailstop 008
P.O. Box 549110
Waltham, MA 02454-9110
781-736-3075
781-736-3107 fax

DATE DUE

Demco, Inc. 38-293